A Time to Break Down and a Time to Build Up

Steps for Moving Forward

SARAH BETH BEVERS

WESTBOW
PRESS®
A DIVISION OF THOMAS NELSON
& ZONDERVAN

This book is a work of non-fiction. Unless otherwise noted, the author and the publisher make no explicit guarantees as to the accuracy of the information contained in this book and in some cases, names of people and places have been altered to protect their privacy.

WestBow Press books may be ordered through booksellers or by contacting:

WestBow Press
A Division of Thomas Nelson & Zondervan
1663 Liberty Drive
Bloomington, IN 47403
www.westbowpress.com
844-714-3454

Because of the dynamic nature of the Internet, any web addresses or links contained in this book may have changed since publication and may no longer be valid. The views expressed in this work are solely those of the author and do not necessarily reflect the views of the publisher, and the publisher hereby disclaims any responsibility for them.

Any people depicted in stock imagery provided by Getty Images are models, and such images are being used for illustrative purposes only. Certain stock imagery © Getty Images.

Scripture marked (ASV) taken from the American Standard Version of the Bible.

Scripture quotations marked (ESV) are from the ESV® Bible (The Holy Bible, English Standard Version®), copyright © 2001 by Crossway, a publishing ministry of Good News Publishers. Used by permission. All rights reserved. The ESV text may not be quoted in any publication made available to the public by a Creative Commons license. The ESV may not be translated in whole or in part into any other language.

Scripture marked (WEB) taken from the World English Bible.

Scripture quotations marked (NASB1995) taken from the (NASB®) New American Standard Bible®, Copyright © 1960, 1971, 1977, 1995 by The Lockman Foundation. Used by permission. All rights reserved. lockman.org

Scripture marked (KJV) taken from the King James Version of the Bible.

Scripture marked (NKJV) taken from the New King James Version®. Copyright © 1982 by Thomas Nelson. Used by permission. All rights reserved.

Interior Graphics/Art Credit: Sarah Beth Bevers

ISBN: 978-1-6642-8952-9 (sc)
ISBN: 978-1-6642-8953-6 (hc)
ISBN: 978-1-6642-8951-2 (e)

Library of Congress Control Number: 2023900989

Print information available on the last page.

WestBow Press rev. date: 02/16/2023

FOREWORD

You can read a lot these days about the concept of mindfulness and how practicing it can equip us, no matter where we find ourselves, with tools to navigate this life more successfully. For some of us and for myriad reasons, the process of completely opening our souls for introspection can be terrifying. Ownership and action are most likely to be difficult and painful. And so it has been for Sarah.

This workbook follows Sarah's story. Minimizing it, it is safe to say her journey has been rough. To know her journey and then to know the woman she is today is profound. This is the chronicle of Sarah's life, her soul laid open for the world to see. It is brutally honest. For me, it is shocking and painful but also illuminating.

With the grace of God, Sarah is healing and living a love-filled, positive, and productive life. I think part of her healing is *this* work. Above all else, what comes through in this workbook is Sarah's love for God, her love for people, and her desire to help them live their best lives.

For those of you who think you are not in need of what she offers in this book, you must think again. For you who deeply (or not-so-deeply) know you need healing, this workbook may be the guide that you are looking for. I challenge you to read it, work it, do it, and live it.

No matter where you are on your journey, this workbook can show you the way to your most healthy and grateful life.

Peace.

—Ellen P. Monica, dear and trusted friend

For everything there is a season, and a time
for every purpose under heaven:
a time to be born, and a time to die; a time to plant,
and a time to pluck up that which is planted.
A time to kill, and a time to heal; a time to
break down, and a time to build up.
A time to weep, and a time to laugh; a time
to mourn, and a time to dance.
A time to cast away stones, and a time to gather stones together;
a time to embrace, and a time to refrain from embracing.
A time to seek, and a time to lose; a time
to keep, and a time to cast away;
A time to rend, and a time to sew; a time to
keep silence, and a time to speak;
A time to love, and a time to hate; a time
for war, and a time for peace.
What profit hath he that worketh in that wherein he laboreth?
I have seen the travail which God hath given to
the sons of men to be exercised therewith.
He hath made everything beautiful in its time: also he hath set
eternity in their heart, yet so that man cannot find out the work
that God hath done from the beginning even to the end.
I know that there is nothing better for them, than
to rejoice, and to do good so long as they live.
And, that every man should eat and drink, and
enjoy good in all his labor, is the gift of God.
(Ecclesiastes 3:1–10 ASV)

This book is dedicated
with love
to my momma,
the woman who taught me how to love
by teaching me about Jesus Christ.

For I know the plans I have for yeus declares the Lord,
plans for welfare and not for evil, to give you a future
and Hope. Then you will call upon me and come and
pray to me, and I will hear you. You will Seek me and
find me when you seek me with all your heart.
(Jeremiah 29:11–13 ESV)

PREFACE

Why should you listen to me?

First off, I bet you are wondering what qualifies me to write such a workbook. Why should you listen to me in the first place? I totally understand that because that's what I always wondered about anyone who tried to give me advice. I don't want you to have to go that route. I want you to have a better go at life than I did. If I share with you my own secrets and my own answers to my problems, perhaps you will be encouraged to work hard to face some of your own problems. I will share what helped me through the most horrible times and the steps I took to get out of my rut and do the work necessary to stay out.

I was at rock bottom. I had been arrested by the FBI, detained as a flight risk, and sentenced to a treatment center. I had nothing but the clothes on my back. My only friends were much like me and facing similar issues. My time in treatment was very lonely. I had nothing to do but think. I was forced to think about and recognize all the addictions, struggles, and problems that I alone had gotten myself into. I came to realize that, throughout most of my life, I had listened to no one. I had shunned all advice, and I had acted independently. I came to realize that anything I learned, I learned by making mistakes, some of which almost cost me my life. This is a sad place to live and a very difficult road to travel.

Creating this workbook was a step in my own healing, and I know it can help anyone who is truly ready to do the work. It won't be like what I had to do, which was to learn the hard way. I took three steps to a new life, and you can take them too:

Step 1: I recognized my need.

Step 2: I understood why I had to have each experience.

Step 3: I found my purpose through those experiences and help others.

I share my full story in part two of the book.

How the process worked for me

Glory to God for all He has done in my life! I cried out for help, and the Lord God came to my rescue. I said a simple prayer asking the Lord to take away the drugs and impulsive behaviors. Three days later, He rolled away the rock. December 12, 2006 was the day I started my journey into recovery.

I am now more than fifteen years into my recovery. I am narcotic free and balanced in my eating and mental disorders. I am a master health and wellness trainer with specializations in corrective exercise and behavioral change through the National Academy of Sports Medicine. God continues to bless my life every day has I grow in Him. I have a wonderful marriage with a man who loves the Lord and his family very much. My husband brings me joy every day, and I am truly grateful for him. I am blessed to have two beautiful sons as well. They are amazing, and I am so proud of them and who they are becoming.

I have a successful career through which I get to help people every day. Not only does my training help my clients to correct their movements and reduce pain and physical weaknesses; I also help them with their mindsets and coach them through their journeys. In helping others, I too am helped, and I can be a blessing back to God.

ACKNOWLEDGMENTS

A Time for Gratitude
Those special people—I thank you!

Marshall, you are the most important person in my life, and I am blessed to be able to spend my life with you. I am truly grateful for you and all you are. I am so amazed at your ability to fix anything and solve any problem. I know that everything is handled when I am with you. No one can do what you do, and I know it. I love you, babe, with all my heart. Thank you for always supporting me and for always being an amazing dad and friend. I like you big time.

I thank God every day for you both, Noah Sebastian Lucas and Travis Corban. You both are the reason my heart knows how to love and why I work so hard. You both have taught me what unconditional love is and how God truly feels toward us as His children. You guys help me serve God more because I want to please God the way you both please me. I am so blessed to be your momma. I love you both very much, and I can't wait to see what God has planned for both of you.

I am so grateful to you, Momma, for being there when no one else wanted to be. You took me in when I was at my lowest and gave me every bit of support that I needed. You have been the best partner through life that any daughter could ask for. You have been the one constant in a life full of uncertain change. I could always count on my momma to pick me up, dust me off, and assist in the takeoff. You have always helped out in all the major projects in my life, and I dedicate this entire project to you and everything you have taught me. I love you, Momma, and I want to thank you for being you from the bottom of my heart.

Thank you, Pappa Joe, for teaching me how to have a servant's heart. You are the most giving man; you give all you can and never judge anyone. I loved getting to know you and understanding you. I am thankful that you came back into my life when you did. God's timing was right; He gave you to me when I needed you. Thank you for always supporting me even when you knew I had made a wrong decision. You loved me through all the bad and understood me along the way. I love you, Grandpa Joe, and I am thankful my boys and I have you.

Mimi, you are the best mother-in-love a woman could ask for. You and Popi took me in as your very own and loved me all the way. You took in my son as your own and supported everything I was working on in my recovery. You never made me feel as if I was broken or damaged and not worthy of your son. You never doubted me when I was doubting myself, and you supported me just as my own momma has done. From day one as your daughter, I have felt just that—the love of a good momma. Thank you for all your help with my postpartum days and for coming over just to let me sleep and make sure my baby digestion was set. I appreciate how you have mentored me in all the right ways and helped me grow in the Lord and in my marriage. Watching you and Mr. Travis made me want to have a happy marriage that would last. I love you, and I am so thankful for you in my life.

Thank you, Josh, Halley, Tyler, and Felisa. I am so blessed to have an extended family who love and respect each other. I am thankful for our family dinners and the fact that all our kids are growing up together and enjoying life in this beautiful country life we have been given. Our bond is truly a blessing from God, and I am very grateful. I love you all so much.

I want to thank you, Nate, for always believing I would stay the course. Thank you for taking such good care of our son and protecting him at all costs. Thank you for not giving up on me and giving me so much support through my recovery. I appreciate you more than words can express. You and Lisa are the reason our families were able to stay strong and grow in a coparent fashion. Thank you!

Thank you to all my siblings. I love you all, and I am thankful that you are in my life. I am thankful for the power of forgiveness and love through Christ.

I have a special thank you to you, my beautiful Sarahs. I love you both, and I am so thankful for you both. You know it all, and you love me anyway. You two have seen me at my worst, and you still love me the best. We will forever be The Trifecta requesting a triceratops at the restaurant. Thank you for being the best of friends and for sticking this life out with me as my people. I love you more than words can ever express.

Thank you, Tracy, for being a wonderful friend to me daily. It isn't often we get a chance to make such close friends as adults. I am grateful for the long talks we have and the studies we share. It is nice to have a friend who is interested in all the same things I'm interested in and who doesn't mind being completely honest with me. I love that we teach each other things as we are learning them and connect on a spiritual level as well. You truly are a gift, my dear friend, and a wonderful sister in Christ. I love you, sis. Thank you for being you.

A special thank you to Jay and Janice Pledger, who first were wonderful clients and then turned into close, supportive friends as well. Thank you for your generosity and wisdom when it can to creating this book. You have been such an inspiration to me, and I pray I will be able to help many people because of what I have learned from you. I will forever appreciate your gracious donation to make this project a possibility. I love you both very much!

A very loving thank you to all my wonderful clients whom I get to work with daily. I am so thankful for you and all the wisdom I gain by working with you. You all push me to be a better trainer. I love you all and appreciate you very much!

MENTORS MATTER,
AND I HAVE HAD THE BEST.

Thank you to the wonderful people in my life who took the time to nurture me and mentor me. They have all taught me so much. I made it my mission to learn something new every year since I started my recovery, and these people certainly started me on my way or have kept that mission alive. Thank you with all my heart.

- Risa for mentoring me in my marriage and taking time to guide me through what the Bible says about a heavenly marriage.
- Pastor David for hearing my testimony and showing nothing but love and respect. You demonstrated what it looks like to shepherd a church family. Under your study, I was able to understand the Gospel in a way I had never done before. Thank you for your leadership in my family's life and in my husband's upbringing. I thank God for the wonderful guidance he was given by the church body.
- Debi Pearl for writing the book that changed my life and my views on marriage.
- Chalene Johnson for mentoring me through organization, creating goals, marketing a successful business, managing my health, and forever serving and teaching your lifers. You have shown me that, when I serve my community, I am serving God. Thank you for all you do. You strive to help everyone as you go. I love you, sis.

- Ashley Sweeney, RD, for your mentoring in health and wellness for my family. Learning from you in your Phase It Up motivational program has been a life-changing experience, and I am thankful for your continuing support. I love watching your family grow; we are blessed to be pen pals.

- Gilda for all of your support in my recovery and for introducing me to my husband. You are the reason my husband asked me out, and I am thankful that you put in a good word for me. Thank you for your support when I first moved to Brenham; it really meant a lot that you listened. Thank you for mentoring me in so many ways. I love you, and I am very grateful that you and Brent are in my life.

- Kimberly and the staff at Fulshear Ranch Academy where I worked for years for mentoring me and giving me a chance after I got out of treatment. I will forever be grateful that I was blessed with that position so I could help those who needed it. Being a mentor for the community taught me how to be a leader in recovery and how I could be of service to others who might be hurting.

- A special thank you to all the women that I worked with at FRA. You were a powerful influence in the beginning of my recovery. Being included in the groups and listening to all your stories motivated me in my own walk. I love you all very much and hope we can always stay white van besties!

PART ONE

Taking Strong Steps Forward

Section One

Introduction

This workbook will help you realize your value in Christ and guide you as you work through the steps to help you understand that God has a plan for your life and an answer for everything you have gone through.

In part one of this workbook, I share with you the steps I took in my recovery from mental disorders, eating disorders, sexual confusion, trauma, and multiple addictions. These are the steps I took to let go of control in my life and let God take the wheel so that I did not have serious problems in my relationships and in my work. These are the steps I took to grow into the woman I am today. I am grateful for the blessings that God has given me. I want to show you how I used these steps to grow and bear good fruit.

In part two of this book, I present my story and I share my testimony about how God has moved and performed multiple miracles in my life. I will share my personal trials and struggles, how I survived them, and how I then found my purpose by working the steps that are in this workbook. There is a part two because I wanted to leave you with the hope that God keeps His promises, and you will have victory in Jesus if you put your trust in Him. God healed me and will do the same for you.

It has been my experience that, when I try to live my life without any guidance, especially godly guidance, my life gets messy. Many times, God has shown me that He is (or should be) the One behind the wheel. In writing this book, I wanted to make sure that God's glory is the most powerful part of this entire workbook. As you will be able to see, Jesus is the One who has always been there and rescued me from every mess I put myself in. It's just as He promised in the Scriptures. I have always been the type of person who must see for myself, experience for myself, and feel for myself. Jesus had to show Himself to me for me to "get it." God answered specific prayers to reveal Himself to me in ways that affirms the truths in the Bible.

How will this workbook help you?

This workbook asks questions that will help you succeed by helping you figure out what is holding you back. You will address the different circumstances you have been through, good and bad, and learn how to turn those circumstances into "your thing" that can help other people. You will be working on your purpose, deciding how you will choose to live your life from this point on. As you work through this workbook and answer each question honestly, you will be able to reflect on the things that happened in your life and how to respond and handle different situations in the future. You will then identify the situations that might trigger you or keep pushing you back into destructive behavior. You will then use those situations to figure out how they can be used to help others.

When you discern your purpose in Christ, you will be unstoppable! Keep this workbook with you. As you recognize situations that create emotions—good or bad—record them here. There is extra journaling space throughout this book. Please feel free to brain dump all over this book. This workbook should be written in; it's meant for scribbling! This reflection will draw you deeper into your own behavior and help you prepare a positive response should you later find yourself in a negative situation. Please use this as a guide for your journey through the Bible.

Each of us is given a job on this earth that is meaningful. Each of us is given an incredible purpose through which God has amazing things to show us. All we must do is seek God's face. In Jeremiah 29:13, we read that "you will seek me and find me, when you seek me with all your heart" (ESV). This is a promise that God says over and over throughout His Word. The Holy Word is alive! I am excited for you to get started.

Here are the instructions for making this book work for you:

1. *Get a Bible!* This workbook is designed as a companion to reading the Bible.
2. Read each step and consider how it applies to your life.
3. Take some time to fill in each space with your thoughts.
4. Pray about each answer. There are no right or wrong answers.
5. Be honest with yourself when answering each question and working through each step.
6. Share your answers with a close, trusted friend for accountability and support.

Tips from the author:

Use this workbook as a daily journal and devotional. Spend time going through each step answering the questions fully and honestly. Each step progresses you onto the next task and its challenges. You will get from this journal what you put into it. Do the work.

May God bless you!

SECTION TWO

About the Steps

The steps:

1. Abandon pride: Admit you need help.
2. Trust: Seek out God as you read His word and put your trust in Him
3. Pray: Write out your prayer to God.
4. Commit: Make a commitment to a life in the Lord moving forward.
5. Address: Write out your struggles and negative strongholds. Address your sin.
6. Confess: Ask God for forgiveness from sin, and repent. Be free.
7. Embrace Jesus: Ask Jesus to be the center of your life.
8. Be grateful: Thank God for everything in your life.
9. Forgive: Ask for forgiveness from those you have hurt.
10. Cleanse: Clean up any lingering arguments, forgive others, and start anew.
11. Reflect: Continually do self-checks and daily affirmations.
12. Seek: Seek God in all you do and set Him as the priority.
13. Share: Tell others how these steps help you.
14. Help: Give back by helping others in need.
15. Live: Make God your lifestyle and grow in Him.

16. Plan: Set goals to grow each year in the Lord.
17. Love: Show the Love of Jesus to everyone. Spread His love like seeds.

These steps challenged me through the beginning of my treatment. Some were harder than others, and they were all reality checks. But God brought me through them, and I learned from each one. Most importantly, I learned how to undo destructive behaviors using these steps. This understanding brought meaning and progress to my recovery. Each page you come to in this workbook will present a step along with the meaning through scripture. Take time to reflect on the scripture and what it means to you. Work each step with honesty and true belief that what you are doing is important and meaningful. Even seemingly simple questions are important. Go deep. Explain yourself as fully as possible. I encourage you to read the book of Titus in the Bible where you will find an explanation of how we should behave as well as hints about what is to come. This workbook is biblically based, so dive into the Word as you go through each step.

A passage from Titus reads:

> Training us to renounce ungodliness and worldly passions, and to live self-controlled, upright, and Godly lives in the present age, waiting for our blessed hope, the appearing of the glory of our great God and Savior Jesus Christ, who gave himself for us to redeem us from all lawlessness and to purify for himself a people for his own possession who are zealous for good works.
>
> (Titus 2:12–14 ESV)

Continue your reading in Titus 3:

> For we ourselves were once foolish, disobedient, led astray, slaves to various passions and pleasures,

passing our days in malice and envy, hated by others, and hating one another. But when the goodness and loving kindness of God our Savior appeared, he saved us, not because of works done by us in righteousness, but according to his own mercy, by the washing of regeneration and renewal of the Holy Spirit, whom he poured out on us richly through Jesus Christ our Savior, so that being justified by his grace we might become heirs according to the hope of eternal life. The saying is trustworthy, and I want you to insist on these things, so that those who have believed in God may be careful to devote themselves to good works. These things are excellent and profitable for people. But avoid foolish controversies, genealogies, dissensions, and quarrels about the law, for they are unprofitable and worthless

(Titus 3:3–9 ESV)

SECTION THREE

Identify That God is Real

You were created by an amazing Creator to do amazing things.

The first subject in this book is to guide you to an understanding of the One who created you. Here you can take some time to read about how you were created by God saying it so. God spoke, and you were made in His image.

The Bible tells us:

> Then God said, "Let us make man in our image, after our likeness. And let them have dominion over the fish of the sea and over the birds of the heavens and over the livestock and over all the earth and over every creeping thing that creeps on the earth." So, God created man in his own image, in the image of God he created him; male and female he created them. And God blessed them. And God said to them, "Be fruitful and multiply and fill the earth and subdue it and have dominion over the fish of the sea and over the birds of the heavens and over every living thing that moves on the earth." And God said, "Behold, I have given you every plant yielding seed that is on the face of all the earth, and every tree with seed

in its fruit. You shall have them for food. And to every beast of the earth and to every bird of the heavens and to everything that creeps on the earth, everything that has the breath of life, I have given every green plant for food." And it was so. And God saw everything that he had made, and behold, it was very good. And there was evening and there was morning, the sixth day.

(Genesis 1:26–31 ESV)

Gospel

Now I encourage you go on to the Gospel of John. Here you will begin to learn about our Lord, Jesus Christ. John was a contemporary of Jesus and one of His first disciples. Think of John's Gospel as his journal inspired by the Holy Spirit. May your words be inspired as you pray and ask God to guide you through your steps in this workbook.

John wrote to us:

In the beginning was the Word, and the Word was with God, and the Word was God. He was in the beginning with God. All things were made through him, and without him was not anything made that was made. In him was life, and the life was the light of men. The light shines in the darkness, and the darkness has not overcome it.

(John 1:1–5 ESV)

And the Word became flesh and dwelt among us, and we have seen his glory, glory as of the only Son from the Father, full of grace and truth. (John bore witness about him, and cried out, "This was he of whom I said, 'He who comes after me ranks before me, because he was before me.'") For from his fullness, we have all received, grace upon grace."

(John 1:14–16 ESV)

In this workbook, you are going to find multiple Bible scriptures you can read to learn more about this blessed, wonderful hope that we have in Jesus. Since this book is also a devotional workbook, take the time to open your Bible and dive into the living word of God! All the answers to all your questions are in this Holy book, the spoken Word of the Living God.

Jesus is all powerful, all knowing, and all seeing. He is the beginning of all things and the end of all things. In God's Word, He speaks to us as a close friend who knows the perfect thing to say at any given time. God's timing is a magnificent thing to experience. My hope is that you get to experience this miraculous timing for yourselves.

This is my prayer for you from Thessalonians:

But we don't want you to be ignorant, brothers, concerning those who have fallen asleep, so that you don't grieve like the rest, who have no hope.

For if we believe that Jesus died and rose again, even so those who have fallen asleep in Jesus will God bring with him.

For this we tell you by the word of the Lord, that we who are alive, who are left to the coming of the Lord, will in no way precede those who have fallen asleep. For the Lord himself will descend from heaven with a shout, with the voice of the archangel, and with God's trumpet. The dead in Christ will rise first, then we who are alive, who are left, will be caught up together with them in the clouds, to meet the Lord in the air. So, we will be with the Lord forever.

Therefore comfort one another with these words.

(1 Thessalonians 4:13–18 WEB)

SECTION FOUR

The Steps—Now You Write!

Stepping into your purpose

This is where the writing begins and the growth happens. I pray that God's will be done in your life, and you are blessed with your daily bread through His Word and your fellowship with Him through prayer and devotion.

1. Abandon pride: Admit you need help!

> Pride goes before destruction, and a haughty spirit before the fall.
>
> (Proverbs 16:18 ASV)

He who conceals his sins doesn't prosper, but whoever
confesses and renounces them will find mercy.
(Proverbs 28:13 WEB)

Getting past your own pride and ego and admitting you are a
human who is struggling and who has negative strongholds will help
set you free. We all have sins that we need help overcoming. Identify
that you need help in your life. Write about the areas in your life that
you need help with and want to change.

_____

_____

_____

_____

_____

_____

_____

2. Trust: Seek out God's Word and put your trust in Him.

> We know that all things work together for good
> for those who love God, for those who are called
> according to His purpose.
> (Romans 8:28 WEB)

God will make His purpose for your life known to you when you put your full trust in Him to work in your life. Make a list of your doubts, concerns, and questions about His purpose in your life. Then give the list to the Lord in prayer. God will listen.

_____

_____

_____

_____

_____

3. Pray: Write out your prayer to God.

> Pray without ceasing.
> (1 Thessalonians 5:17 WEB)

Pray to God and ask Him to take the wheel in your life, then write it out in a letter to Him.

When you have a difficult question, situation, or crossroad in your life, commit to the practice of praying to God for direction. Ask Him to guide your path, and allow Him to light your way with truth. Ask Him into your life, and He will do the rest. Write your "prayer letter" to God and rest in Him.

_____

_____

_____

_____

4. Commit: Make a commitment to a life in the Lord moving forward.

> For God so loved the world, that He gave His only born Son, that whoever believes in Him should not perish but have eternal life. For God did not send His Son into the world to judge the world, but that the world should be saved through Him.
>
> (John 3:16–17 WEB)

> That if you confess with your mouth, "Jesus is Lord," and believe in your heart that God raised Him from the dead, you will be saved.
>
> (Romans 10:9 WEB)

Now comes the time to trust in your God and believe He sent His Son Jesus to die to save you from your sin. Make a commitment to believe in and to serve Christ who died on the cross so that you may have eternal life free from death in sin. Commit to choose to follow Jesus and His teachings in your life. This means you become a big fan of Jesus and put your efforts into Him instead of anything on this earth that He created. Choose to worship the Creator and all He says.

You see, nothing—not even death—could not keep Jesus down. He rose again to show that, in Him, we can live. He did this to give you life everlasting. He did this out of love. Give yourself to Jesus because He first loved you. When we let go and give ourselves to God, He can work freely in our lives. He can show us His purpose and place us on the right path. Pray that you will allow Him to move in your life by letting go of anything that you set in place without His guidance or put before Him completely. Ask God's will for your life. Write down your prayer asking Jesus into your heart and your life to guide you and direct you through His Word.

_____

_____

_____

_____

_____

5. Address: Write out your struggles and negative strongholds. Address your sin.

Now the deeds of the flesh are evident, which are: immorality, impurity, sensuality, idolatry, sorcery, enmities, strife, jealously, outbursts of anger, disputes,

dissensions, factions, envying, drunkenness, carousing, and things like these, of which I forewarn you, just as I have forewarned you, that those who practice such things will not inherit the Kingdom of God.
(Galatians 5:19–21 NASB1995)

He has delivered us from the domain of darkness and transferred us to the kingdom of his beloved Son, in whom we have redemption, the forgiveness of sins.
(Colossians 1:13–14 ESV)

Address your sin by doing a deep dive into your life and your behaviors. Make a list of the things in your life that are keeping you from fully giving yourself to the Lord. List the struggles, negative strongholds, and selfish actions that are keeping you from a close walk with Christ. This includes your sins, your disobedience, and the things you put above God. It includes the dirt in your life and the skeletons in your closet. It's time to clean house. We all have sinned and disobeyed God in one way or another. When you make a list for yourself and address these sins with Jesus and ask Him for forgiveness, He will free you from that bondage.

Believe this—Jesus Christ gave His life to atone for our sins. Because of this and because of your faith in Him, you are forgiven. There is abundant freedom when we ask for forgiveness and address these strongholds in our lives. Remember that Jesus came to heal us from our sin. Healthy people do not need healing; He came to heal the sick and weak and brokenhearted. Jesus meets us exactly where we are. He heals those who seek Him for healing. When you become aware of your sins and ask Jesus to forgive you, He will begin to heal the pain caused by these struggles and sins in your life.

Jesus forgives me for ...

_____

_____

6. Confess: Ask God for forgiveness from sin and repent. Be free.

> If we confess our sins, he is faithful and righteous to forgive us our sins and cleanse us from all unrighteousness.
> (1 John 1:9 ASV)

> I acknowledged my sin to You, and my iniquity I did not hide;
> I said, "I will confess my transgressions to the Lord."
> And You forgave the guilt of my sin. Selah
> (Psalm 32:5 NASB1995)

> Therefore, if anyone is in Christ, he is a new creation.
> The old has passed away; behold, the new has come.
> (2 Corinthians 5:17 ESV)

Confess by considering each of the sins in your life you have addressed and asking Jesus to forgive you for them. Then repent of them. This means you turn away and you don't go back to them or let those sins back in your life without addressing them again. You are now free from that sin, and you are forgiven! It is your choice to leave it alone and never go back to that way of life.

When you repent and turn away from your sins and from the old ways, you get to start anew. When you confess them to Jesus, your sins are forgiven; they are gone from your life. You have become a new creature in Christ. Write down your confession prayer to Jesus simply asking for forgiveness from your sins you previously addressed.

_____

_____

_____

_____

_____

7. Embrace Jesus: Ask Jesus to be the center of your life.

> Then Jesus said to His disciples, "If anyone wishes to come after Me, he must deny himself, and take up his cross and follow me. For whoever wishes to save his life will lose it; but whoever loses his life for My sake will find it.
> (Matthew 16:24–25 NASB1995)

> Therefore, prepare your minds for action. Be sober and set your hope fully on the grace that will be brought to you at the revelation of Jesus Christ—as children of obedience, not conforming yourselves according to your former lusts as in your ignorance, but just as He who called you is holy, you yourselves

also by holy in all of your behavior, You shall be holy,
for I am holy.

(1 Peter 1 :13–16 WEB)

Turn to Jesus daily and ask Him to be the center of your life. When you make Jesus the center of your life and follow His teachings, you are less likely to fall back into any bad behaviors or a destructive, sinful lifestyle. Learn who you are in Christ. It is important to spend time working on yourself and learning to do things independently. Know how to be alone with your thoughts and how to handle your emotions in a healthy manner. This is a fantastic time to work on yourself and the way you want to serve God.

If you are single, give yourself at least a year to figure out just who you are in this new way of living before you let someone else into your life and begin dating. Build your friendships and work on these new goals. If you are in a relationship, use this next year to work on prioritizing your relationship and growing together in Christ. Include your partner in your goals. Allow him or her to support you; in return, be sure to show your love and support as well. Keep all your relationships healthy and your communication open and with love. Practice joy with others and in your personal life. That is the best advice I have ever been given. In this space, write about ways you can spend your time growing in Christ. Then write about ways you can build your friendships or future relationships with healthy boundaries, trust, and above all with love like Jesus's love.

Make a list of ways you will make Jesus a priority in your life.

---

8. Be grateful: thank God for everything in your life.

> But thanks be to God, who gives us the victory
> through our Lord Jesus Christ.
> (1 Corinthians 15:57 WEB)

> "In everyhting give thanks, for this is the will of God
> in Christ Jesus toward you."
> (1 Thessalonians 5:18 WEB)

> Enter into His gates with thanksgiving, and into His
> courts with praise. Give thanks to Him, and bless
> His name.
> (Psalms 100:4 WEB)

Make a list of all the blessings that you are grateful for in your life. These can be people, things, feelings, ideas, and so forth. List the ways that you feel blessed in your life. Identifying everything you are grateful for daily and thanking God for your blessings are wonderful way to worship the Lord. He wants us to know He is with us and that He is the one that we should be thanking for everything He has given. Write out your gratitude.

_____

_____

_____

_____

_____

9. Forgive: Ask for forgiveness
from those you have hurt.

> Confess your sins to one another and pray for one
> another, that you may be healed. The insistent prayer
> of a righteous person is powerfully effective.
> (James 5:16 WEB)

> Do nothing from selfishness or empty conceit, but
> with humility of mind regard one another as more
> important than yourselves; do not merely look out for
> your own personal interests, but also for the interests
> of others. Have this attitude in yourselves which was
> also in Christ Jesus.
> (Philippians 2:4–6 NASB1995)

Ask for forgiveness and try to make it right. In this step, you must consider other people and their feelings before moving forward. This step should come when there is a true change in your life and you are far away from those destructive behaviors and hurtful things you are addressing. If possible, without hurting people more, go to the people you've hurt and admit, acknowledge, and apologize for your past behaviors. Do whatever you can do to make amends. Actions speak louder than words, and love can cover a multitude of wrongs. Make a list right here and show each person Christ's love by asking them for forgiveness. Some people are going to need to see a living amendment from you; show them with your life and the way you approach things from now on. Forgiveness is the most healing gift we have been given.

_____

_____

_____

10. Cleanse: Clean up any lingering arguments, forgive others, and start anew.

> Don't lie to one another, seeing that you have put off the old man with his doings, and have put on the new man, who is being renewed in knowledge after the image of his Creator, where there can't be Greek and Jew, circumcision, barbarian, Scythian, bondservant, or free person; but Christ is all, and in all. Put on therefore, as God's chosen ones, holy and beloved, a heart of compassion, kindness, lowliness, humility, and perseverance; bearing with one another, and forgiving each other, if any man has a complaint against any; even as Christ forgave you, so you also do.
> (Colossians 3:9–13 WEB)

> Above all, keep loving one another earnestly, since love covers a multitude of sins.
> (1 Peter 4:8 ESV)

Make a list of people who have hurt you and record how they hurt you. Search your heart to find any resentments you might be holding onto with anyone in your life. Think about the current condition of each of your relationships in your life. Take time in prayer, and ask God to reveal to you the conditions of your relationships as well. If a person has harmed you, don't wait for him or her to apologize. If possible, reach out and offer to squash the problem. Let go of any bitterness and grudges. Wipe the slate clean. Seek to show love to each person. We must love one another just as Christ loves His church. We want to make sure that all our relationships are as good and healthy as they can be. We never want to hold onto resentment or bitterness. When we practice madness and bitterness, we become mad and bitter. When we let it go, God can move in and fill the void with love.

Yes, you've been hurt, and, yes, you have hurt people. But remember, Jesus came and died for our sins. If He Who has no sin can forgive our sins, then we must forgive the sins of others. When you know you are forgiven, you can begin to forgive others. Forgiveness will help you let go of resentment. Asking their forgiveness may help those you've hurt let go of resentments toward you. We always must remember that there are consequences for every action we take. Forgiveness is a holy thing. When there is forgiveness, Jesus can move in amazing ways.

_____

_____

_____

_____

_____

11. Reflect: Continually do self-checks and daily affirmations.

> Examine your own selves, whether you are in the faith. Test your own selves. Or don't you know about your own selves, that Jesus Christ is in you?—unless indeed you are disqualified. But I hope that you will know that we aren't disqualified.
>
> (2 Corinthians 13:5–6 WEB)

Don't be conformed to this world, but be transformed by the renewing of your mind, so that you may prove what is the good, well-pleasing, and perfect will of God.

(Romans 12:2 WEB)

Search me, O God, and know my heart; try me and know my anxious thoughts; And see if there be any hurtful way in me and lead me in the everlasting way.

(Psalm 139:23–24 NASB1995)

Every day do a self-check and reflect on your behaviors to become aware of your attitudes, your priorities, and your responses toward the things around you and going on in the world. Make sure your intentions are pure. Voice your affirmation to do right in the eyes of God. Say it out loud in prayer to God, asking Him to reveal any area that you are not aware of today. Now, write down the areas in your life that you would like to improve and ask God to move in those places daily. One of my daily prayers goes like this:

Thank you, Lord, for my life. Holy Spirit, I ask that you guide me in the way you want me, that I will treat each person I meet with kindness and bless as many people as possible today. Jesus, direct me closer to You and open my eyes to see You today. Spill out of my mouth with love to everyone I meet along my path.

_____

_____

_____

_____

_____

12. Seek: Seek God in all you do and set Him as the priority.

> But seek first the kingdom of God and His righteousness,
> and all these things will be added to you.
> (Matthew 6:33 ESV)

Seek God first in all you do and set your eyes on Jesus as your priority daily. You have put your trust in Jesus to forgive your sins and pray for devotion to God's Word; now it is time to fellowship with Jesus daily. We do this by reading the Bible, listening to His music, and dancing to the Lord in praise. Praise Him daily. Fix your eyes on Him. Decide a plan of action to keep yourself doing this every day. I want you to write the first thing you do each day to get your day started. What is your regular morning routine? Does it start with prayer or time reading the Bible or other study on God's Word? Make God part of your morning routine by including Him in the start of your day.

_____

_____

_____

_____

_____

13. Share: Tell others how these steps help you.

> But we will not boast beyond proper limits, but within the boundaries with which God appointed to us, which reach even to you.
>> (2 Corinthians 10:13 WEB)

> But "he who boasts, let him boast in the Lord."
>> (2 Corinthians 10:17 WEB)

> Thy testimonies also are My delight and my counselors.
>> (Psalm 119:24 KJV)

> Your testimonies are wonderful; therefore, my soul observes them.
>> (Psalm 119:129 NASB1995)

Share your testimony with others. Share how God has worked in your life and use the example of your experiences to help someone who might struggle with similar issues. Shine a light on all that you do by sharing how Jesus saved you from your sin and set you on the right path living with Him. This always helps the people you talk to with their struggle; it is why support groups are so successful for recovery. This is when you will show your vulnerabilities and let people see your authenticity about your story. Pay it forward when God presents the opportunity to share your story with others. Write a list of all the ways working these steps have helped you and use those as your topics as you share your testimony with others. This is the part in the workbook in which you get to identify how God has moved in your life thus far. You get to show the world how God has changed you; you get to help those in need by sharing God's glory.

14. Give back by helping others in need.

> And whatever you do, work heartily, as for the Lord
> and not for men, knowing that from the Lord you
> will receive the reward of the inheritance; for you
> serve the Lord Christ.
>
> (Colossians 3:23-24 WEB)

This is where your purpose comes in. Trust that your Creator, the Almighty God, will lead you in this. When you pray each day, ask God to guide you to be able to bless someone each day just has He has blessed you. You now understand that Jesus has forgiven you for all the times you sinned and didn't rely on Him. You now understand that you cannot do everything on your own. You know what it's like to live without relying on Jesus: Life goes awry. Now that God has rescued and redeemed you, it's time to help others to receive their blessings through Christ.

He uses His believers to follow in his footsteps to help those in need. This happens when you share the Gospel (the good news about Jesus) with them and show others how Jesus works—He works by serving others. Yes, this is the Gospel—the belief that Jesus is the only way. You get to share it with others by doing things like praying for others, exemplifying charity, serving the community, listening to those in need, and providing what they need. You get to plant seeds in their hearts so that they can start to grow on the solid ground of Christ. It's as if you're setting them up with the foundation so that God can help them build the life that He has planned for them. Jesus tells us that not all seeds grow and bear fruit; sometimes seeds fall on rocky soil or among choking weeds. Understand that the entire process can and may take a while. But if you share your loving obedience, you can show people the true love of Jesus Christ and move them toward Christ for themselves. You get to be a part of that. This is when things start getting exciting.

Make a life out of helping others in the same way you were

helped. Whether you volunteer or choose a career that offers a platform for service, prioritizing others will keep you on track. List some different opportunities for you to serve within your community. Make a list of all the ways you can help others in your life. Who is the Lord leading you to so that you can help? This could be within your community, your church, or even within your family and friends.

_____

_____

_____

_____

15. Live: Make God your lifestyle and grow in Him.

Do not be slothful in zeal, be fervent in spirit, serve the Lord.
(Romans 12:11 ESV)

Serve the Lord with gladness! Come into His presence with singing!
(Psalm 100:2 ESV)

Make God your lifestyle and grow in the Lord daily. Walk daily in prayer and fellowship with Jesus and set Him above all other things in this world. Have no other gods before Him—Christ Jesus. List the things you do that you can replace with time with the Lord—with music, with books and studies, with fellowship with other believers, or even with the movies and entertainment in our lives. Does your social media reflect Jesus? Does your attire reflect Him? Would people be able to see the change of Jesus in you?

_____

_____

_____

_____

16. Plan: Set goals to grow each year in the Lord.

> And whatever you do, in word or deed, do everything
> in the name of the Lord Jesus, giving thanks to God
> the Father through Him.
>   (Colossians 3:17 ESV)

Set goals that keep you continually growing, learning, and serving the Lord, your God. Now that you are improving your walk with the Lord daily and sharing what He gives you with others, you are blessed with such a joyful experience; it is God's will in your life. You will get to do great things through Christ who strengthens you. Write out the goals you would like to accomplish. Then pray about them and ask Jesus to guide you and help you discard anything that He doesn't want for you. Jesus shutting a door can also be an answer to prayer. He will always open a new one—or a window! Jesus is your strength. He is your Shepard, and He has plans for your future to prosper. Include Jesus in all your plans. Center your goals around Jesus. Jesus will bless this type of goal setting. List your goals here, and we will learn to sort them out later in the workbook.

_____

_____

_____

_____

_____

17. Love: Show the Love of Jesus to everyone. Spread His love like seeds.

> Jesus answered, "The most important is, 'Hear, O Israel: The Lord our God, the Lord is One. And you shall Love the Lord your God with all your heart and with all your soul and with all your mind and with all your strength.' The second is this: 'You shall love your neighbor as yourself.' There is no other commandment greater than these."
>
> (Mark 12:29–31 ESV)

Spread love to everyone you meet. Pray for good intentions toward everyone before every door that you walk through. Make every encounter a meaningful one. Embrace each moment and be present with those around you. Listen to others in a way that meets their needs. Look out for other people first and share your experience and help when needed. This is a good time and place to think about and record your intentions for your relationships. This is a good time to think about the boundaries you will set. And this is the time and place to articulate just how you want others to treat you. Making of list of these things will help you in all your relationships because you will be able to communicate your actions and feelings with more clarity. It will help you lead with love.

_____

_____

Continue

If your actions are guided by these seventeen steps, you will begin to see the purpose God has for your life. By going through hard times and struggles, we are more equipped to help others through theirs. God wants us to examine ourselves as you have by following these steps. When we can continue this way of life and repeat these steps with any struggle that life might throw our way, we are walking with our full armor of God, and He can continue to move and work in our lives.

> I know that You can do everything, and that no
> purpose of Yours can be withheld from You.
> (Job 42:2 NKJV)

This is where you can brain dump your thoughts. This is some extra journaling space for you to use if you had more to add. You could always make a list of things that you would like to work on or accomplish for your future.

_____

_____

_____

_____

_____

SECTION FIVE

A Time to Heal, a Time to Grow— Questions to Ask Yourself for Deeper Healing and Awareness

To be aware is to be alive!

Set yourself up for success by knowing what obstacles you may face. Answer these questions and have these areas in your life addressed before they happen. You will then be better prepared for how you may act or react to different situation that happen in life.

But recall the former days when, after you were enlightened, you endured a hard struggle with sufferings, sometimes being publicly exposed to reproach and affliction, and sometimes being partners with those so treated. For you had compassion on those in prison, and you joyfully accepted the plundering of your property, since you knew that you yourselves had a better possession and an abiding one. Therefore, do not throw away your confidence, which has a great reward. For you have need of endurance, so that when you have done the will of God you may receive what is promised. For, "Yet a little while, and the coming one will come and will not delay; but my righteous one shall live by faith, and if he shrinks back, my soul has no pleasure in him." But we are not of those who shrink back and are destroyed, but of those who have faith and preserve their souls.

(Hebrews 10:32–39 ESV)

These are the questions that I was asked to help me identify my triggers and enable me to develop a plan of action and prayer to use when these areas come up in my life. Each question is designed to get you thinking and to bring awareness to the areas that need your attention. This step in the process is essential if you want to develop a relapse prevention plan that will keep you moving forward and keep you from ever falling backward in your sinful behaviors. Get honest with yourself and write down everything that comes to mind. Keep this list of questions and come back in six months to see if your answers have changed or if anything is clearer to you. This is a cool place to see how far you have come. This is where you take a deeper look into your core issues and really start to know yourself and how you want to behave when difficulties come up. This is where you learn to cope with issues that might upset you by turning to Jesus and resting in the Lord through scripture and prayer. You will find your greater purpose by answering the following questions and then writing out a list of actions that can replace those past destructive behaviors. Resolve how you want to respond in the future. In your Bible, you will read in Psalms 119, a song of praise and encouragement, as you work through these next questions and scriptures.

In this section, we will be talking about these core issues:

1. Triggers
2. Prevention
3. Family
4. Connection
5. Memories
6. Fears
7. Comfort
8. Inspiration
9. Struggles
10. Setbacks

1. Triggers

> And the peace of God, which surpasses all understanding, will guard your hearts and your minds in Christ Jesus.
>
> (Philippians 4:7 ESV)

What are the people, the places, or even things that upset you and cause you to want to act out in those past behaviors you addressed in the first set of steps? It could be something that you hate to deal with in life that causes you to respond in a negative way.

An example: "Every time I go to Austin with my friends, I want to ..." Or "Whenever I see so and so, I get depressed and ...."

Make a list of these possible triggers that come to mind and might put you into a negative headspace.

_____

_____

_____

2. Prevention

> Beloved, don't be astonished at the fiery trial which
> has come upon you to test you, as though a strange
> thing happened to you.
> (1 Peter 4:12 WEB)

> Count it all joy, my brothers, when you fall into
> various temptations, knowing that the testing of your
> faith produces endurance. Let endurance have its
> perfect work, that you may be perfect and complete,
> lacking in nothing.
> (James 1:2-4 WEB)

What are some different ways you could respond to the people,
places, and situations that cause you to want to react impulsively in
a negative way? With what can you replace any relapse-inspiring
behaviors? Make a list of possible solutions or ways you can protect
yourself from heading back into destructive behaviors. Walking
away from a situation or place is always a safe option. It might
just be a simple prayer; write that prayer here as a reminder. Set
up the plan and resolve it with actions. What is your plan if all
your buddies want to go out partying? What is your plan if you
encounter drugs again? What is your plan if your body wants to
binge eat or emotionally eat? What is your plan if times get hard
and you get sad and you get depressed and you fall into a relapse
cycle? Knowing what you're going to do and who you're going
to call is a great line of defense. Set up a plan so that you are less
likely to fail when times get hard. But remember first and foremost
to cry out to God for guidance and ask Him to take control of
your life. When you add Jesus to the equation, you guarantee a

greater outcome. Trials and tests will come in this world; those are the situations that refine you into gold, and God can use you for His glory.

_____

_____

_____

_____

_____

3. Family

> Children, obey your parents in the Lord, for this is right. "Honor your father and mother" (this is the first commandment with a promise), "that it may go well with you and that you may live long in the land." Fathers, do not provoke your children to anger, but bring them up in the discipline and instruction of the Lord
> (Ephesians 6: 1-4 ESV)

Describe your relationship with your parents, your guardians, or the adults who raised you as well as your siblings and extended family members. Are you in contact with them or able to visit them often? If your relationships with them are healthy, continue to make them better buy describing how they are now and where you those relationships to grow. If there are problems that are keeping the communication blocked or the relationships strained, write about it here and start to work on mending those things.

_____

_____

_____

_____

_____

4. Connection

Finally, all of you be like-minded, compassionate, loving as brothers, tenderhearted, courteous, not rendering evil for evil or insult for insult; but instead blessing, knowing that you were called to this, that you may inherit blessing.

(1 Peter 3: 8–9 WEB)

What are some of the ways you can try to connect better with your family members and even close friends? What are your solutions to anything that you addressed in the previous step? Though you may be dealing with family resentment and past hurt and maybe even guilt and shame, God wants you to walk in forgiveness and compassion first. Jesus loves us first, and we need to walk in that way for others to show others Jesus in our lives.

_____

_____

_____

_____

_____

5. Memories

> Indeed, if a man should live many years, let him
> rejoice in them all, and let him remember the days
> of darkness, for they will be many. Everything that is
> to come will be futility. Rejoice, young man, during
> your childhood, and let your heart be pleasant during
> the days of young manhood. And follow the impulses
> of your heat and the desires of your eyes. Yet know
> that God will bring you to judgement for all these
> things. So, remove grief and anger from your heart
> and put away pain from your body, because childhood
> and the primes of life are fleeting.
> (Ecclesiastes 11:8–10 NASB1995)

What are your first memories and thoughts about your childhood or upbringing? Do you have any lasting memories that you never want to forget, or maybe some thoughts you had about different subject you learned as a child? It could be your favorite vacations, friends, activities, or foods. It could also be things you disliked or that upset you has a child; things that would set you off or cause you to act out. Maybe it is something that your parent or guardian did that you liked or disliked—something you want for your children or maybe something you never want for your children. Did you get in trouble a lot? For what? These are all questions to help you get started.

Sometimes remembering different experiences can help us understand why we behave in certain ways, and we can learn more about ourselves. This exercise helps us to be more aware of things that might trigger us to return to a negative place or experience a negative reaction. Addressing these issues may get you thinking about different situations that you could identify with, so you can help others in the future by understanding stuff you learned in your past. Answering some of the questions will help you learn from your past as well and will help you learn how and why you do what you do or like what you like. Recalling is a great tool for understanding how and why certain things happen in our lives.

_____

_____

_____

_____

_____

6. Fears

> Anxiety in a man's heart weights it down, but a kind word makes it glad.
> (Proverbs 12:25 WEB)

> In nothing be anxious, but in everything, by prayer and petition with thanksgiving, let your requests be made known to God. And the peace of God, which surpasses all understanding, will guard your hearts and your thoughts in Christ Jesus.
> (Philippians 4:6–7 WEB)

What are you afraid of more than anything? Maybe it is something you say you will never do, or something that triggers fear or anxiety whenever you think it or are faced with it. These may be painful times in your life that hurt to think about, but God is faithful to give us peace to replace these fears. Address these fears and painful areas to God, and He will be your comfort in times of need. God is doing healing work in you, and He sent us Jesus as the Great Healer in our lives. The Bible tells us so in many scriptures.

_____

_____

_____

_____

_____

7. Comfort

For God didn't give us a spirit of fear, but of power, love, and self-control.

(2 Timothy 1:7 WEB)

The Lord is near to the brokenhearted and saves the crushed in spirit.

(Psalm 34:18 ESV)

Heal me, Lord, and I will be healed; save me and I will be saved, for you are the one I praise.

(Jeremiah 17:14 NASB1995)

Write down some other scriptures that comfort in times of fear and anxiety or any time you need comfort in your life. These words will comfort you through the presence of Jesus in your life. Instead of relying on those different comforts and vices that we used in our destructive sinful behavior, we now have the promise of God's comfort in our lives. God's word is His comfort to us always, and in His word, He says He is with us always. He wants us to have peace in Him.

_____

_____

_____

_____

_____

8. Inspiration

For we are his workmanship, created in Christ Jesus
for good works, which God prepared beforehand, that
we should walk in them.
                    (Ephesians 2:10 ESV)

And we know that for those who love God all things
work together for good, for those who are called
according to his purpose.
                    (Romans 8:28 ESV)

Ask and it will be given to you; seek and you will
find; knock and the door will be opened to you. For
everyone who asks receives; the one who seeks finds;
and to the one who knocks, the door will be opened.
                    (Matthew 7:7–8 NASB1995)

With inspiration, you can set your priorities and goals in
accordance with your new way of living. God tells us He knows the
desires of our hearts, and He wants us to prosper for His glory; we
must trust Him and tell Him the desires of our hearts in fellowship
and prayer with Him. God desires that from us. God has given us
many talents and gifts, and when we take time to set our goals in line
with Christ and those talents, we will work with joy. When we shine
a light that others see and want to know about, we will inspire them
to seek out where our joy comes from. What do you want most out

of your life? What do you desire your life to be more than anything else? What makes you unstoppable? Maybe this is what drives you to keep going; maybe this inspires the accomplishments you hope to achieve. What are the elements in your life that bring you the most joy? That is where I would start.

_____

_____

_____

_____

_____

9. Struggles

Behold, I am with you and will keep you wherever you go and will bring you back to this land. For I will not leave you until I have done what I have promised you.
(Genesis 28:15 ESV)

With him is an arm of flesh, but with us is the Lord our God, to help us and to fight our battles." And the people took confidence from the words of Hezekiah king of Judah.
(2 Chronicles 32:8 ESV)

The Lord is my rock and my fortress and my deliverer, my God, my rock, in whom I take refuge, my shield, and the horn of my salvation, my stronghold.
(Psalm 18:2 ESV)

I can do all things through him who strengthens me.
(Philippians 4:13 ESV)

The righteousness of God through faith in Jesus
Christ for all who believe. For there is no distinction.
(Romans 3:22 ESV)

The wisdom of the sensible is to understand his ways,
But the foolishness of fools is deceit.
(Proverbs 14:8 NASB1995)

A wise man is cautious and turns away from evil, but
a fool is arrogant and careless.
(Proverbs 14:16 NASB1995)

What are your biggest daily struggles? What sins keep coming up in your walk? What areas of your life do you find the most difficult to accomplish on your own? This could be your patience, anger, codependency, or addiction. It could be your lust, an idol you put before God, or any sin in your life that you are having a hard time releasing. It could be other kinds of struggles that keep you from accomplishing your goals like time management, communication, or money management. Maybe you want to change something about the way you start or organize each day. How are your boundaries with your friends? Do you allow toxic people to dominate your day? Do you let people run your life, or are you the one who pushes people around and throws fits? What does your character look like? How are you when no one is watching? Do you exhibit dignity? Dignity is defined as the state or quality of being worthy of honor or respect. God is here to restore our dignity and clothe us in it with His strength. If you are stuck in a rut that you can't seem to cross, this is where you can confront it and lift it up to Jesus in prayer. This is where Jesus will take all your struggles and make them your strengths.

_____

_____

_____

_____

_____

_____

_____

_____

_____

10. Setbacks

that He would grant you, according to the riches of His glory, to be strengthened with power through His spirit in the inner man, so that Christ may dwell in your hearts through faith; and that you, being rooted and grounded in love, may be able to comprehend with all the saints what is the breadth and length and height and depth, and to know the love of Christ which surpasses knowledge, that you may be filled up to all the fullness of God.

(Ephesians 3:16–19 NASB1995)

Are there some other areas in your life that are holding you back? Maybe there are skills that you haven't learned. Maybe there is something you keep trying to do on your own, but you know you need assistance. Is there anything of your life that is holding you back? Is there anything restricting you? Education, money, time, mindset, health, or your support system are all good areas to look at when answering this question.

11. Mission

Here is The Great Commission Given by Jesus:

And Jesus came up and spoke to them, saying, "All authority has been given to Me in heaven and on earth. Go therefore and make disciples of all the nations, baptizing them in the name of the Father and the Son and the Holy Spirit, teaching them to observe all that I commanded you; and lo, I am with you always, even to the end of the age.

(Matthew 28:18–20 NASB1995)

Write out your mission statement. This is your promise to yourself that will guide your future life. How will you treat all aspects of your life going forward? How do you want to treat people? How do you want to be seen by the people around you? A good mission statement defines your purpose, your values, and the goals of your daily walk or even your business. This statement will set you on the right track each day and help you see your goal in relationship to everything else in your life. You are setting priorities with this statement. Here are some good examples of what a mission statement can be, keep it simple so you can write it and remember it.

"I put Jesus in the center of my life and seek to bless and inspire others to do the same."

"I aspire to walk in kindness and help as many people as possible each day."

_____

_____

_____

SECTION SIX

Time to Plan and Set Your Priorities and Goals

Now it is time to set yourself up to grow an awesome, successful life for yourself in Christ. Now that you have set your mission statement for your life, expand on that with your prioritized goals and dreams for your future.

Pray about these goals and for whatever you want for your life. God knows and sees the desires of your heart. He has plans for you to prosper, and He wants you to be happy. Talk to your Father and tell Him what you want your life to look like. He will let you know how He can help you achieve the life He has planned for you. If you seek Him, He will show Himself to you.

Answer each question about your priorities and goals. You will then be set up with the steps you need to take to move you closer toward your goals. Break your large goals into smaller, achievable goals that will move you closer to your large goals for your future. Take these goals one step at a time and one day at a time, and make sure they match up with your values and priorities.

Write out the way you want your life to look and feel in the future. Get creative and imagine your best life. This is your big dream, your big picture, the things you desire to achieve.

_____

_____

_____

Prioritize

> Do not be conformed to this world, but be transformed
> by the renewal of your mind, that by testing you may
> discern what is the Will of God, what is good and
> acceptable and perfect.
>   (Romans 12:2 ESV)

Be sure to synchronize your goals with your top priorities and core values. When we prioritize the things that are the most important for us to focus on, the goals we make for ourselves will come together with our priorities in focus. Simple as that. You will not be easily pulled off your focus if you plan.

What is your thirty-day priority? What are the things that you want to focus on most in your life for the next thirty days?

Make this your top priority; it will help everything else fall into place. Here are ten areas for you to keep in focus during this transformational time in your life:

1. Your walk with God (daily devotion and prayer with the Holy Spirit)

2. Your mental and physical health
3. Your environment at work and at home
4. Your passions and hobbies (the things that bring you hope and restore you)
5. Your romantic life
6. Your social life with family and friends
7. Your finances (Do you have a budget in place and are you giving back?)
8. Your work or purpose in life (Are you doing what you love or making the best of it?)
9. Personal growth through seeking wisdom (reading literature from elders and Holy Word)
10. Your service (mission work or community outreach)

What needs the most attention in your life right now? I recommend prioritizing the items in this list from one to ten in order of importance to you. Which one do you feel you are focusing on now and doing well? That one is number ten! You are on top of this in your life! The area that needs the most attention is number one. When you are finished reorganizing, you will see that the areas near the top of the list are the ones that you must focus on and keep tabs on the most right now. You need to improve in these areas. There are possibly multiple areas that need your attention. That is perfectly okay, and you will improve in all of them if you focus on them.

Write down the top three areas that need your attention right now.

1. _____

_____

_____

2. _____

_____

_____

3. _____

_____

_____

Set goals

> I press on toward the goal for the prize of the upward
> call of God in Christ Jesus.
> (Philippians 3:14 NASB1995)

> For where your treasure is, there will your heart be also.
> (Luke 12:34 ESV)

Update your priorities and your goals every thirty days to make sure you stay on track for reaching your goals with good intentions. Make sure that you set your goals to match up with the things that you have prioritized in your life previously. This process enables you to set goals that line up with your prioritized core values.

Some things to consider when setting goals for yourself and creating a plan of action.

Are you setting SMART goals for yourself? Ask yourself these questions about each goal you set.

1. **S**pecific: Is this a specific goal that matches my priorities?
2. **M**easurable: Is this a measurable goal?
3. **A**ttainable: Is this an attainable goal for me?
4. **R**ealistic: Is this a realistic goal for me?
5. **T**imely: Can I get this goal done in a timely manner?

For example, there is no way to measure progress if your goal is "to get healthy." But setting a goal that you will lose ten pounds by a certain reasonable date is something that you can measure.

Are you pushing yourself outside of your comfort zone with your goals? You must be challenged to really change.

Are you setting positive goals? Set goals that will yield positive effects in your life. Your goals should push you toward your top priorities.

Your minor goals should get you closer to your major goals overall and keep you balanced and focused on your top priorities. Take this time to set yourself some SMART goals. Ask yourself those five questions about goals before you write down anything and your goals will be easier to accomplish.

I encourage you to write about everything that comes to mind that you hope to accomplish in the next thirty days. This is something that you will recheck and redo every thirty days to keep you consistent with this positive behavior, which will help you in your growth.

> Whoever pursues righteousness and kindness will
> find life, righteousness, and honor.
> (Proverbs 21:21 ESV)

Now pick your top three goals that you want to hit in the next thirty days:

1. _____

   _____

   _____

2. _____

   _____

_____

3. _____

_____

_____

Organize: a time to set up

A good way to get started working on the goals you've just set is to know what you will need to achieve each one:

- Will it take time?
- Will it cost money?
- Will you need to be more self-controlled?
- Do you require more education or knowledge?

Identify the requirements for each of your top goals and go deeper in what is needed to get the job done. So many times we start a goal only to lay it aside because we don't set up for success. These simple steps will set your intentions in the right directions and keep you focused on what is needed for each task you have ahead. Write down what is needed for you to accomplish your first three goals and then come up with a plan for each goal. God will supply everything you need to accomplish His purpose for you. He has brought you through all these steps, and He will supply if you are willing to do the work He requires.

_____

_____

_____

SECTION SEVEN

Support

A time to seek help

One of the best ways to hold yourself accountable for your actions and continue in this positive way of life is to seek help and a support system. This can keep you going when times get hard and your mindset begins to shift. Instead of letting your mind feel attacked by enemy thoughts, have a person or an organization lined up to contact and then a direct line there. Seek out support to help you achieve the resolutions that you discovered in this journal. There are many resources to help and keep you on track. Please know that you are not alone, and God is always with you.

Here is a list of great resources for you to check out in your community for support.

- Therapy with a counselor. (Focus on the Family's Christian Counselors Network is a great resource: https://www. focusonthefamily.com/get-help/ 1-855-771-HELP [4357])
- Loving supportive spouse
- Treatment center for detoxing and getting well
- Church group
- Pastor
- Trusted friend
- Family member

- Support meeting or sponsor
- Mentor
- Literature to keep you on track and motivated
- A new environment
- Volunteer program at a charity or church

It is good to give back to the community. Try to surround yourself with positive, like-minded individuals who will support and love you. This will keep you grounded. Turn away from negative and toxic environments. Love others but surround yourself with strength and positivity so that you can support and help others who are also struggling. You need positive support and positive influence in your life in order to achieve this. Make a list of the people and places that you would like to change and replace them with positive people and a positive environment. Keep negative people at a distance; you will be strengthened in the process.

_____

_____

_____

_____

_____

SECTION EIGHT

Study

A time to grow and bear god's fruit, a time to study Jesus

In this section, you will learn how to study God's word and establish a daily routine for journaling and keeping up with your daily devotion to Jesus.

It is important to listen to or read the Word of God daily to be encouraged. It is important to know what is expected of you by your Creator. It is important to be knowledgeable about the oldest and most preserved books ever put together. Once you start really listening and studying and having an ear to hear, you will gather wisdom to understand—I mean really understand—what God is saying to you. When you make this a daily routine, you can get excited about diving deeper and learning more. The one place you can always go to for love and support is the Holy Word of God. Using the Bible app YouVersion (https://www.youversion.com/the-bible-app/) is a great way to have a daily devotion with God, even when you're on the go. There are also online Bible websites (https://biblehub.com/, https://www.biblestudytools.com/, https://www.biblegateway.com/. Or, of course, you can use your nondigital Holy Bible. Whatever format you choose, just dive right in.

The verses I list in this section are good for exploring and understanding as you begin your walk with God and your journey to find your purpose. Even if you were to study one of these scriptures a day, your effort would be beneficial in helping you and confirming what you are doing along the way.

Writing out the verses or your thoughts about a verse will really help. These verses are just a start. Reading them will get you into the Bible; hopefully you will be interested to learn more. Use the other spaces in the journal to write out other verses that you like or that have helped you through different situations. You can also write out your thoughts and feelings to keep you thinking about what you have read.

Proverbs 28:13

_____

_____

_____

1 John 5:16

_____

_____

_____

1 John 4:20–21

_____

_____

_____

James 1:20

_____

_____

_____

Colossians 3:13

_____

_____

_____

Ephesians 4:1–32 (Take a few notes on this one; it is good!)

_____

_____

_____

Galatians 6:1

_____

_____

_____

Galatians 6:6

_____

_____

_____

Romans 12:1–21

_____

_____

_____

Ephesians 2:8–9 (Saved by faith.)

_____

_____

_____

Romans 10:9

_____

_____

_____

Titus 3:5

_____

_____

_____

Act 4:12

_____

_____

_____

John 14:6

_____

_____

_____

John 3:16–21

_____

_____

_____

Acts 16:30–33

_____

_____

_____

Acts 2:38

_____

_____

_____

Mark 16:16

_____

_____

_____

Romans 5:8

_____

_____

_____

2 Corinthians 5:21

_____

_____

_____

John 5:24

_____

_____

_____

John 11:25–26

_____

_____

_____

1 Thessalonians 5:9

_____

_____

_____

Revelations 3:20

_____

_____

_____

Now faith is the assurance of things hoped for, the conviction of things not seen. For by it the men of old gained approval. By faith we understand that the worlds were prepared by the word of God, so that what is seen was not made from things which are visible.
(Hebrews 11:1–3 (NASB1995)

An arrogant man stirs up strife, but he who trusts in the Lord will prosper.
(Proverbs 28:25 NASB1995)

So, the churches were being strengthened in the faith, and were increasing in number daily.
(Acts 16:5 NASB1995)

Put on the whole armor of God, that you may be able to stand against the schemes of the devil.
(Ephesians 6:11 ESV)

Grow up Spiritually!

Therefore, leaving the elementary teaching about the Christ, let us press on to maturity, not laying again a foundation of repentance from dead works and of faith toward God.
(Hebrews 6:1 NASB1995)

Whoever says he abides in him ought to walk in the same way in which He walked.

(1 John 2:6 ESV)

To put off your old self, which belongs to your former manner of life and is corrupt through deceitful desires, and to be renewed in the spirit of your minds, and to put on the new self, created after the likeness of God in true righteousness and holiness.

(Ephesians 4:22–24 ESV)

For by grace, you have been saved through faith, and that not of yourselves; it is the gift of God, not of works, lest anyone should boast. For we are His workmanship, created in Christ Jesus for good works, which God prepared beforehand that we should walk in them.

(Ephesians 2:8–10 ESV)

Now the works of the flesh are evident: sexual immorality, impurity, sensuality, idolatry, sorcery, enmity, strife, jealousy, fits of anger, rivalries, dissensions, divisions, envy, drunkenness, orgies, and things like these. I warn you, as I warned you before, that those who do such things will not inherit the kingdom of God.

(Galatians 5:19–21 ESV)

The penalty for disobedience or sin is death, and separation for God forever. For the wages of sin is death, but the free gift of God is eternal life in Christ Jesus our Lord.

(Romans 6:23 ESV)

PART TWO

*My Personal Testimony and
How These Steps Worked for Me*

INTRODUCTION

In this part of the book, I will share with you my story—how I worked these steps, and how they worked for me. I believe it is important for you to hear how God moved in my life and helped me through everything I experienced. My testimony is to help you understand how you can learn from your experiences and even help others use your experiences as a guidebook for the start of their own personal journeys on the same path.

I limited my narrative to my outlook and what I can personally remember through experience. I have not included the names and identities of family members. This is a look into the personal thoughts and emotions I experienced as I grew up and all the ways God worked in my life. This part of the book is to give Jesus all the glory; it is my thank you letter to Him.

> For by grace you have been saved through faith; and that not of yourselves, it is the gift of God; not as a result of works, so that no one may boast.
> (Ephesians 2:8–9 NASB1995)

> But sanctify the Lord God in your hearts. Always be prepared to give an answer to everyone who asks you to give the reason concerning the hope that is in you, with humility and fear, having a good conscience. Thus, while you are spoken against as evildoers, they may be disappointed who curse your good way of life in Christ.
> (1 Peter 3:15–16 WEB)

CHAPTER 1

The Before

Well, here I am sitting in the back of a federal SUV with the handcuffs tight against my wrist. I've just been arrested by FBI SWAT. I can't move an inch, my nerves are going haywire, and my mind is running wild. All I can think about is the meth in the bathroom cabinet at home and the certain sense of relief that I had no drugs with me when I was picked up. I know that it is over, and I know that there is no going back. I know that this is my chance to get help. This long drive to the federal building from North Austin has me overthinking everything that just happened and what got me to this point. My inner thoughts are at rapid fire: *Well, this is it. I'm going to tell the truth about everything. From this point on I know that there will be no more lying. There will be no more cheating, there will be no more hiding behind anything. I have to come clean; I have to plead guilty. Who will pick my son up from school? What is he going to think of me? This is one way to get clean. How did I even get myself into this?*

As far back as I can remember, I attended church with my momma. I was taught the Word of God and the ways of Jesus. I was taught that I get all my strength from God and that He is protecting me and providing for me. My mom became a Christian when she was in her late twenties and wanted to start a new life in the Lord when she became a mother. Being born again as an adult is like relearning everything you ever knew and giving up an entire past life to live for the Lord. My mom grew up in a military family; she lived in multiple places all over the country and didn't get any spiritual teachings as a child. She never stayed in one place long enough to make long-term friendships. So, once she became a Christian, she wanted to know everything there was to know about her new Christian lifestyle. She spent her time around fellow Christians trying to learn. She attended Bible lessons and church meetings as she tried to understand what God wanted for her life.

Twice on Sunday and once on Wednesday evening every week, my siblings and I attended church with my mom. Rain or shine, we were going. And, on the way, we picked up neighbors to take with us. My mom wanted to help as many kids learn about the Lord as she could. We stayed at the church until the last person left because my mom oversaw the cleaning of the facility and locking up. She was the church custodian. I really enjoyed my Sunday school teachers and the people at our church. There we experienced a sweetness that we did not experience at home.

At home, my mom was newly married, and we had just moved to a new town closer to our stepfather's family. A new home and new life, new family, and new everything. I remember this as a confusing time, especially at the beginning of the marriage. I remember there being a new sense of power and control in the house. Life was hard for us for many years because of this new life. The challenges for a man who marries a single mom can be more than anticipated, especially when one child is hyperactive and has sensory issues. (That would be me.) There was an attempt to take over the home by power and control, forcing and orchestrating everything in its path. Meals were a focus for control, and there was zero patience for any emotion.

The people at the church helped us stay strong in the church; they involved my mom in all the departments. She was the children's church director, and we all participated in vacation Bible school every summer and Christmas plays every winter (she directed the shows). Our church community was a sort of safe place where I could learn and express myself through all the fun activities, we got to be involved in.

I was the kind of kid who asked adults lots of questions in a very frank way. I questioned everything that I learned at our church. I did feel the love of Jesus, and I did believe that He was a man who lived a perfect life because He is God's son. I asked Jesus into my heart, and I was baptized in 1987 when I was seven years old. I continued to learn more at different Bible camps and day camps for girls. I attended youth camps and then later did mission work. All the while, I was struggling with a confusing home life and struggling with my body image and sensitivities to the things around me.

One day, there was a wakeup call for my mom that exposed what was going on within the family. After that, my mom insisted that something change, so we moved. I know that my mom tried her hardest to protect us when she found out the power and control that had taken over the home, and it ended abruptly. Overnight, we moved. My mom packed us up and moved us away from the trouble and into a new home that was all ours. For me, it was confusing time because I didn't know how to feel about any of it.

During this time, I was dealing with personal experiences that were confusing everything in my life. Some of the older neighbor kids introduced sexual behaviors and began performing sexual acts on me and around me. This continued for years and really affected me emotionally. We rented the house where this all started, so I moved into the room where it all happened. It was a strange time in my life because, at nine years old, I was sexually active with both an older girl and an older boy. This had been going on for a while before the divorce. I was struggling in many ways. My sexuality was the most confusing part of my existence. I was attracted to both males and females, and I felt as if I didn't belong around either. I had trouble with female friends because I would get clingy or feel out of place and then I would either get rejected or I would run away from the friendship with a new friend and pray the same thing wouldn't happen with this one. I never told anyone I was dealing with these feelings and emotions. I just kept it all in and felt like an outsider all the time. I began withholding food from myself and hating my reflection in the mirror. I started to rely on addiction to love and to food, and I combined the two. One day, for example, I stayed home from school and ate an entire pizza, but instead of swallowing it, I'd chew it up and spit it out while watching soap operas. I was nine years old and indulging in some weird behaviors. I later learned that I was trying to establish control over my life when everything else was so uncontrollable and confusing.

I began to rebel against all authority. I thought I knew everything. I felt like an outsider wherever I went. I felt that I knew more than the other kids. They were all just living such weak lives under their parents' control. I, on the other hand, was living an independent life under my mom's roof. I had a key to the house, and I came and went as I pleased. I was the girl who had a weird home life with no dad.

This sort of life can really affect a kid. But I can tell you that I never felt as if I could judge anyone's home. I was dealing with so much at my house, everyone else's house was awesome. I was always friendly to all the kids at school, and I can say that I had friends within each clique. But felt as if I didn't belong to any of them. I had two close friends in high school, and we did everything together. I am still the best of friends with one of them today. We have been close since we were thirteen years old. I love that woman!

I had many best friends as I was growing up, but never at the same time. I would be really close to someone and then, suddenly, the relationship would become strained. I can only think of one friend who was with me ever since we became friends—my best friend Betty. She has always helped me through the toughest times, and I will be forever grateful that God placed her in my life. I always felt that I was a steppingstone best friend with people until they found out how weird I was and then moved on to the cool kids or I did something bizarre to push them away. Betty Boo never made me feel that way; she stood by me and cared.

In junior high, I engaged in solo activities, so I really didn't have to be with a team. I didn't want a team to have to rely on me. I hated people watching me do things for the first time. It made me completely anxious. I did try out for the mascot, and I made it. I loved it. I could dance around "in disguise" being a crazy vibrant person expressing myself physically. I could do whatever I wanted under that costume, and I didn't feel as if anybody was watching me. I felt free. Dancing was what I was supposed to do, so I could act a fool and just completely stem out. I got to do this without anybody knowing what a release it was for me.

I had a costume box as a kid, and every day after school, I would dress up and stay in character until I was told to take the outfit off. I was a cat every day for a year! I was so hyperactive that my mom had to find ways for me to release my energy. She wouldn't let me come inside on pretty days. I had to ride my bike and play outside every day to get that energy out. If I was too jumpy, I wasn't allowed to play video games. She signed me up for tap dance lessons, and I would tap dance all over our garage. When my mom felt I need to be punished, she would make me write sentences, or should I say paragraphs. Or she would make me stare at the toys that I couldn't play with. Mostly I was punished because I couldn't sit still and listen to the sermon at church. Mom had to find creative ways to teach me how to focus and concentrate because I was a wild woman. I now know what that was all about, but as a kid, I was just the crazy one that should be medicated. I am so thankful that my mom did not go that route and that she did teach me coping skills like riding my bike, dancing, and writing.

I was born with my feet kind of twisted to an extreme "pigeon toe." The doctors put my feet in the correct position and placed me in casts up to my thighs with a bar between them. I was in these casts for the first six weeks of my life. After the casts, I had to wear corrective shoes. My mom would even put my shoes on the wrong feet to encourage them to grow and form the right way. No wonder I was a hyperactive child, I was finally free to move!

Today, as an adult, to keep my hyperactive brain tame, I lift weights, do exercises and yoga stretches, and of course, dance around my house. These activities help me to keep my energy levels normal. I also make sure I stay away from processed foods, sugars, and dyes.

It's such a blessing to have knowledge that can help me to do better in all ways.

At the age of ten, I finally was properly introduced to my dad, and he was suddenly back in my life after he had been living away on the streets of California. It is a crazy side story, but one that I must tell. I was denied contact with my biological father after my first visit with my new stepfather at age three. I didn't have contact with him except for the dumpster diving treasures he sent me in the mail and the occasional phone call. During these calls, I was coached through the entire conversation. I was told to say, "Can my daddy adopt me?" Of course, I didn't know at the time that I was crushing my biological dad's spirit even more and thus causing more confusion and distance between us. I could feel all the pain during every call, so I ran away from all of it. I do remember getting an awesome shelf with cool cubbies for books and toys in the mail from my dad. He had built it himself. My dad is a carpenter and a painter and a very creative man. He can paint characters, so he would make money on the streets painting the windows of businesses during the holidays and decorating houses. He would also pick up cans and sell them. He gave cans and blankets to other homeless people on the street as well. He told me lots of cool stories about how he helped people. He believed he was doing God's work during the time when he was homeless. I am glad he got away from it all so he could live a strong healthy life for himself.

At age ten, when I was in fourth grade, I met my dad. I was getting ready for school, and I heard a knock at the door. I opened it to a long-haired John Lennon type with the tiny glasses and everything. He walked right in and said very loudly, "Honey, I'm home!" My mom, from the other room yelled, "Joe?" I shoved my entire fist into my mouth. I was floored. What had just happened? I saw no car or taxi, just a bag.

Apparently, when my mom got divorced, she had sent a letter to my aunt who lived in California near my dad. He was told that he could come visit, and that mom was divorced. He loaded his van with all his dumpster-diving treasures and headed to good ole

Texas. Well, the axle on the old van couldn't handle his load, and it broke before he even left California. He left it and hitchhiked a ride with a trucker who was headed to Dallas. I'm sure he told this trucker his whole life story—how he hadn't seen his kids and wife in years and finally had a chance to visit. The trucker drove him all the way into the little town of Podunk, Texas, and dropped him off in front of our house in the middle of the night. So, my dad got into the back of our station wagon and slept there until the sun came up. When he heard us talking and awake, he knocked on the door.

My mom had my dad's van towed from California and thought his being with us was a good thing. For three months, he lived in our driveway in that van, slowly moving things into the garage and then into the house. He worked on his relationships with us kids and my mom. One day, they sat us down around our wooden kitchen table and told us that they were getting remarried, and Dad was moving in. I do remember asking her not to do that, but I know now that raising kids alone is one of the most stressful things a person can deal with. I believe that, from her point of view, she thought she was doing the right thing. My dad was and is a good man who never harmed her, so she thought he would help her. I know that we all have our shortcomings, but he tried to redeem himself by coming back to help.

Shortly after they got married, we planned a trip to see my grandmother and then go on vacation with other family members. We never made it to that vacation. My grandma passed away the afternoon before we were supposed to leave on the trip. I was watching *The Smurfs* on television when I was told that my grandma had died. I was told to go outside and wait for the ambulance. It was such a weird time in my life. Right after my grandma passed away, our family really became divided; her death caused a huge separation within the family. I was no longer able to see family members I was very close with and loved very much. It was as if that part of the family wasn't part of our family anymore. All communication was broken. It was very sudden, and it was a very sad time.

Grandma's funeral was the first funeral I ever attended, and I was very thankful that I had my dad around during this time. I felt as if we had a connection; I finally had my father with me when I needed him. I followed him around and watched every move he made. He told me he loved it and that I reminded him of a little puppy. I was just so curious about him. I was desperate for a father figure who wanted me around. *I'm here for the first time ever and have my daddy with me!* I was beyond excited but still confused and guarded. I still didn't feel as if I could tell him anything or get too close to him, but I did still feel that I had something special. Well, at least for a little bit. The marriage lasted only three years—just enough time for them to buy a beautiful log cabin in the country and for us to get settled as a family together. Sadly, he then left, and they divorced. They'd had such a volatile past together, and that affected any future they would have had.

We hated to move back into a rental house back in town, but we did it. We started over again with just my mom. We were back in solo mode. My mom was back on her own, and she was a fighter. She never gave up. She always worked five jobs or so to support us kids. She also put herself through college and got a bachelor's degree in psychology. She had a great job as an executive director. I am very proud of how my mom took care of business when times were hard for us. She is the reason that I am so independent and self-sufficient. She made a lot of tough decisions. Some were the right ones and some were the wrong ones, but she never stopped fighting and supporting her kids. I am so grateful for my mother and her strength and for her ability to overcome so much adversity. She always worked hard to keep us involved in church and with good, positive friends. I know that, if my mom hadn't been so supportive, I would've had it much harder. I would have been an angrier person with a lot more emotional problems. My mom really did keep us together with some strong glue. It was a little bit like crazy glue, but it was strong glue.

Mom opened a coffee shop in town and ran that business with some great partners and great friends who eventually let her buy the entire business and take over. She loves to bake, cook, and to serve people food, so this was her dream job. She gave me a job with a lot of responsibilities. This gave me the opportunity to make a little money and learn about a good work ethic. That's one thing that her father had taught her. My grandfather was a command sergeant major in the army, and he retired after twenty-four years of service. My mom learned how to work from him. She devised a list of chores. Each one was dependent on another. Then she handed out assignments that forced us to learn how to work with one another. Even if we were fighting, we could work with one another to get our house in order. I can tell you that this strategy has helped me so much throughout the years in all my jobs and all my relationships.

Well, while my mom was building her first coffee shop, she was also being pursued by a gentleman she'd met at church. This was happening when I was sixteen, and I didn't care about men or anything that my mom was doing. I didn't care about her getting remarried or anything that wasn't about me. I did think it was good that she met him at church. I felt someone like that would be a better fit than someone who didn't believe the same way mom did. I just let her do her own thing and didn't try to offer any input. I was the normal teenager. I had a job, a boyfriend I was infatuated with, and a great school and social life. I was always distancing myself from my family. I was active in the church group and with all my church friends, yet I was running around and doing whatever I wanted with my boyfriend. I was so unbalanced in my thinking toward relationships. I felt the need to control any situation that I didn't like. I didn't want my boyfriend to smoke or drink, but we could have sex and sneak around. I lied to my mom and snuck around to be with him, but I forced him to meet me at church every Sunday morning and every Wednesday night. I was also struggling with power and control with my food. I would binge and purge daily and exercise because I hated my body. I worked two jobs and stayed busy all the time. My goal was to stay away from my house and become my own person. I struggled in church with the fact that I was having all these problems, so I confided with a group leader about everything. She tried to use me as an example in front of the whole youth group, but I wasn't having it. I gave the whole church the middle finger and left, never to return. I loved God, but I disliked Christians. I didn't trust them anymore.

CHAPTER 2

The Fall

The summer before my senior year in high school, I got into a fight with my boyfriend because he was going to move to California without me and leave me in Podunk, Texas. He was a year ahead of me in school, so he had just graduated and wanted to travel before starting any kind of college education. I broke up with him and adopted an "I do what I want when I want" attitude. I started partying before and after work with coworkers. I started doing drugs, and I eventually failed a drug test at school. I was told I couldn't graduate with honors anymore and that I couldn't be a part of any extracurricular activities. I had to withdraw from the National Honor Society, the Who's Who of America, and from being an athletic trainer. That sounded boring, and school was the last thing on my mind, so I was done. I decided to finish school with an Operation Graduation program. I finished my credits in two days of testing. I then moved to Austin at the beginning of April in 1999. I had gone to visit the summer before my senior year and had a blast. So, when it came time to move, I was set up with a roommate right away. I just went back to school to walk across the stage later when everybody else graduated.

In Austin, I got a job at a pizza parlor. Eventually I got a better job at a big computer company where I earned too much money for an eighteen-year-old. I worked late and went to all kinds of awesome places to eat and watch all kinds of shows. I had a blast! I did anything and everything I wanted. Talk about independence. Or was it? I was codependent on boys, drugs, music, art, and keeping up with the entire city. I would go way too far with my decisions, and then I would be reminded of how much God loves me whenever He saved me from a dirty situation. It was as if He would reel me back in and protect me with a shield. It was very apparent that I survived only because of God's will in certain situations. One night, I nearly died from an overdose of pills when I was nineteen. I prayed out for help and made it through the night. I then realized how fleeting that life was.

I sought out a change; I needed something different. I asked my high school boyfriend to take me back and marry me, and he did. Talk about codependent. I was also very impulsive and just acted on a whim daily. This was just another example of me just taking control and trying to manipulate the situation to serve a purpose for myself. We had an apartment together in North Austin, and my mom thought it would be best if I moved home so that we could plan the wedding together. I was very fortunate that I could carry out my job over the phone in a private office, so I was able to move and continue working. I moved back home and planned the wedding. Three months later, when I was only twenty, we were married.

All was good. I seemed content. I was popping pills and still partying when I got the chance. I did have Christian counseling before I got married, but I didn't do anything for God. I didn't deny Him anymore either. I lived a very flesh-driven life, and I still did what I wanted. I would hang with friends and go to shows and parties with or without my husband. I was still on drugs (pain pills at this time), still struggling with eating disorders, and keeping everyone in the dark about it all. No one knew my weird little secrets with food and with drugs. I thought I was hiding it from everybody. No one ever acted as if they knew, so I just assumed they didn't. In my mind, that was just a permission statement to keep going. Then the unexpected happened. I got pregnant!

CHAPTER 3

The Next Level

We didn't plan this pregnancy, and it scared me to my core. I cried and got very depressed. I stopped the drugs immediately, but I turned desperately to the food. I was purging everything that wasn't healthy. I was crazy about nutrients for the baby, but I was binging on junk food and getting rid of it. I did this just to turn around and eat something healthy for the baby. I didn't start to show until I was seven months along. I have crazy stretch marks because of this. My skin was not able to stretch properly and gradually. Ladies, don't do this!

Once my son was born, I felt that I had a purpose. I was absolutely in love with this new little man. I wanted to be the best mom I could be for him, but I still had a lot of unsolved issues. I suffered from postpartum depression and didn't know how to do all the "mom stuff." I felt helpless and tired and then lazy and then crazy!

I hated my body, and I wasn't losing the baby weight. I was tired all the time, and I worked for a preschool. I was decorating the classroom on an off day, and just like that, a coworker gave me a line of the stuff right there on the changing table. Cocaine—a big line of it! Let's just say that things spiraled out of control very fast. This coworker would come to my home after work to use and then supplied me with friends who introduced harder stuff. Before I knew it, I was completely dependent on substances to take care of all the postpartum problems. I can honestly say that I became addicted to a drug that I never even paid for. It was given to me every single time, and then I became dependent on it. This did not take long. I used it every single day. These people who were very close to me handed it over to me on a dosage basis. They say misery loves company; it is no joke. I guess I was fun to be around, and I was even more fun when I was on the drugs.

The situation became out of control very fast. I did leave my husband so that no one ever saw me using drugs and so that my uncontrollable addiction wouldn't hurt anyone. My ex-husband and my child were never exposed. We lived like roommates with a child, and I took that as my excuse to separate myself from him. I thought that this would keep him from getting hurt as well. I was living a very sinful life and making very sinful choices, and I knew that if I stayed with him, I would just hurt him and everyone in my path. So, I left. This was when the real hurt began. I had a separate apartment in the same apartment complex so that I could keep my habits secret and try to keep everybody safe. Now that is a clear indication of some serious power and control problems if you ask me.

I thought I had control over everything until I lost control of everything and anything. I'll let you in on the end. I lost my job. My car was repossessed. I was moving from apartment to apartment; I was getting evicted as if it was a hobby. I was destroying relationships with family members and friends. I was causing pretty much everything around me to fall apart. I had gotten myself into a hole that I didn't know how to get out of without the extreme help of others. I was in some real darkness. It's insane how far the Lord will allow you to go before He calls you back.

I am so thankful for my ex-husband during this time because he was a fantastic father and took wonderful care of our son. He allowed me to see him but always took care to put him to bed and stay the night with him. He was a homebody, so it worked out well, and I took advantage of that. I regret the way that I treated my family. I am so thankful for the grace of God and the mercy of my family for forgiving me for all these many sins—making everything in my life fall apart: my relationships with family members, my husband, and friends who didn't want me going down that path. So many people tried to stop me, but at the same time, my closest friends were giving me drugs for free. I was selfish and pulled away from my family to keep living the life I wanted. I was following the "high life," and I was gross.

CHAPTER 3

Rock Bottom

I lived with another boyfriend who was a musician. He knew tons of other artists, so we went to concerts every night. I met lots of different band members, and in my mind, I thought I was living the life. We were behind the scenes during tours and got to hang out with the members of all the bands. But it was all fleeting, and I was so high that I would often not remember how we got home. I met people that I don't even remember meeting. So many other people in Austin were using drugs partying the way I was, so I was able to maintain this lifestyle for quite some time. It was as if I was chasing some high that wasn't attainable. My ex-husband seemed happy and content with his girlfriend, and they were the primary caregivers for my son. I was gone all the time to shows. I was very selfish with my time, and I just did whatever I wanted. My husband filed for divorce and started a new life with his girlfriend. They gave my son the environment that I was not mentally able to give him. I was able to maintain a façade that I had nothing to do with my son's upbringing or that I was even a mother. I distanced myself from him. I was so strung out, and I am thankful today that my son has no recollection of that person I used to be. I am thankful for the role that my ex-husband's wife played in my son's life. She took in my son as her own and loved my family when I was very mentally ill. I appreciate her even though, at the time, I gave her my worst.

I struggled with everything in my life including maintaining a home to call my own. I was unable to keep a job, a car, an apartment, a lasting relationship, or even friendship with someone who could trust me. I was manipulating the system at all costs to survive. I was breaking all kinds of laws to live the life I wanted to live. I was running scams, stealing, dealing drugs, committing fraud, breaking and entering, stealing cars, and doing many more things that I am not proud of having done. So, lost, so alone, and so addicted to so many drugs, I was helpless and hopeless, depressed and dying. I weighed ninety-two pounds and was running from everything, including God. I wished that He couldn't see me. I didn't want anyone to see me, especially not my son. Yet, he was all I could think about and longed for. His father had removed him from my presence long before I had got myself to this point, and I am very thankful that he did. My son was able to have great memories of that time; he was not involved in the terror I was dealing with mentally. I had no real home; I had been evicted from four different apartments in one year. I even lived out of a moving truck for months. I slept on people's couches and was literally homeless for about a year. Sometimes I did not know when my next meal was going to be. People were always giving me drugs, and that also turned into feeding me. I was like a little stray animal roaming around different apartment complexes. I would build relationships, suck the people dry, and then get evicted. I would manipulate any situation serve myself. I got what I wanted when I wanted it. This was an enabling life for me. It was a criminal life. I was making criminal decisions; I was not to be trusted. I couldn't control myself any longer. I am so thankful that I didn't end up with multiple charges for petty things throughout all this time. I am also thankful (and surprised) that I didn't get killed.

God really protected me from my behaviors at this time because He had me going down for something bigger, something that would last and something that would help me for my future. Oh, I know how He was working, and I can see that now looking back. I have journaled about all this time in my life, and I have received help through therapy and counseling. I can now take a step back and really see how much God shielded me. He allowed me to go through so much darkness so that I could clearly see what truth really looks like. I can tell the difference between the two lifestyles. I also know how to help others who are struggling in all these areas. I can live without judging anyone—ever!

CHAPTER 5

The Surrender

In 2006, my lifestyle caught up with me. I had had enough of living off people. I was sick and dealing with so many mental issues. My use of drugs and my own selfish ways were dictating my every move. I was sick and tired of being so sick and tired, and I knew it all had to change. I did have an opportunity to change locations and try to get clean on my own. I was living with a guy at the time, and my mom offered to let me move in with her. She wanted to help by moving me back to the small town where she was living. The boyfriend I was with was probably done with all my manipulating and was more than happy to pack me up in his truck. He drove me an hour and a half to my mom's house. He unloaded my stuff and said good-bye. I don't think I've seen him since. That's what happens when you use people; they take as much as they can bear, and they don't mind letting you go. I lived with my mom for three months. I did a lot of art; I did a lot of exercise and a lot of nothing. The whole time, I was popping anxiety pills to stay calm. I wasn't getting clean by any means.

I started working for a woman down the street helping her with housework and errands while she recovered from surgery. I knew I had a problem when I could not resist her pain medication. With the first paycheck she gave me, I bought a car with some cash I had saved so I could leave town. I packed some things for an extended stay and booked it to the last place I lived. I thought I needed to get out of town before I did something that would give my mom a bad name. That's how I knew I needed help, but I just ran from the situation.

I ran to Austin and got a job working for the retired captain of a big biker gang and his crew. I worked managing the house. I was paid good money weekly, and I was given room, board, and a nice car to drive. On the outside, I appeared to have it all together. Oh, yeah, I was also fed all the drugs I could handle. They were musicians so they traveled all over and played music at different dive bars. There was inherited money, so they were pretty much independently wealthy. Even though I had what looked like a good life, it was so unhealthy and destructive. I was getting to visit with my son, and I was able to pick him up and do things with him a couple of times a week. In the beginning of December that year, I had a Christmas tree, and the whole house decorated for Christmas. There were even presents under the tree.

But there was something wrong. There was something terribly wrong in my life. I was still addicted to meth and all kinds of pills and whatever else people put in front of my face for me to use. I was a poly-substance druggie, and I could not go very long without using some sort of heavy narcotic, psychedelic, or pharmaceutical drugs. My favorites were stimulants. Combining all of them was a habit of mine. The only time I wasn't using was when I got to be with my son, and I loved that feeling of being with him. I would visit for only a day at a time, and I could wait till he was gone before I was back on the drugs. I followed every unholy activity and lustful temptation my mind got set on, and I was full of pain in my emptiness.

I needed help. I did not know how to stop my self-destructive behavior on my own. I was fed up. I called out in a prayer for God and asked Him to take the drugs out of my life. I wanted a good life away from all the self-destructions. I looked at my meth pipe, then I took a bath and went about my day. Little did I know that God was listening, and He would be sending help.

Three days later, I was stopped dead in my tracks by FBI agents! Oh yeah, before I had moved to Brenham and back to Austin to live with the bikers, I had received a call from a federal government agency. They needed to speak with me, but I just ignored that call and did not go in for that briefing. I just pretended I never received that call, and I guess I thought it was just something I could hide away from. But the federal government is better than that.

So, on that day, I had just gotten high on both meth and marijuana, and I felt I needed to go outside and top off with a good old Parliament Light cigarette.

This was my rock bottom day. I was being arrested for crimes I had committed the previous year—not the petty little stuff I had been doing to survive the day to day, but a money crime that involved eight other people and a half a million dollars. A man I knew had been dolling out checks that were owed to people who had mineral rights on some land in Arkansas. He manipulated the system and put in people's information so that we would receive payments in the mail to split with him. He involved quite a few people and kept us all secret from each other. This was a good thing because we were looking at a conspiracy case with a minimum of ten years imprisonment.

So there I was sitting in the back of a federal vehicle surrounded by federal agents and overthinking my entire life and wondering how I had got myself into the mess and what was going to happen now. I was helpless and letting go of everything I had been doing. As crazy as it was, and as scared as I felt at that moment, I knew that my prayers had been answered. God had pulled me right out of that toxic environment and set my feet on steady ground. I had never shown up to that meeting, so in their eyes, I was a flight risk. I was a fugitive who had not complied, so a warrant had been issued for my arrest. When I moved back to Austin, let's just say my whereabouts were known by a close friend and codefendant who reported me to the FBI.

CHAPTER 6

The Help

On December 12, 2006, I was placed into custody in a county jail cell and detained for seven days while I waited for a place for me to open at Austin Traditional Center, a residential treatment center and halfway house.

When I was first arrested, I was given a lawyer who tested my urine. A judge addressed the result of the test: there were multiple substances in my system at the time of my arrest. I confessed and asked the judge for help with my drug problem. My request was granted. I was sentenced to ninety days in pretrial residential treatment. While I was at the center, I worked my program and began to work my steps with a sponsor. I prayed to God, asking Him to give me strength. I admitted that I was a sinner and an addict. The first step in the workbook was the start to all the help I received.

When I was in treatment, I prayed for Jesus to come back into my life and take control of my life. I decided to surrender my life to God. If I didn't, I was going to die in my addiction. I knew that if I went back out to use drugs, I would die.

I began to work my twelve steps of Narcotics Anonymous (NA) and write out my life story. I began to figure out what my core issues were and that my problem was with my self-image and control issues. Why did I always turn to my addiction to food, drugs, or sex and relationships when I was feeling stress, discomfort, or anxiety? Why did I want to change the way I felt in some way all the time? Why had my life been driven in this way for as long as I could remember?

I learned that I didn't know how to cope with anxiety; indeed, I didn't know how to cope with any of my emotions. I learned that this was because I had lived through multiple stressors as a child that had caused several kinds of disordered thinking. I learned these during treatment. It took lots of hard work with counselors and professionals and working the steps in the workbook you hold in your hand. None of it was easy. Every single second was scary, especially living in a dorm with a bunch of other women. Plus, I never knew what the next move in my legal situation would be or what the next court date would entail.

I struggled with my eating disorder throughout my treatment and even after I got out of treatment. I got rid of the drugs, but I was having trouble maintaining a healthy body image and a healthy mindset toward my body, which had been damaged from so many years of disordered behaviors. A lot of time and a lot of work and a lot of different disciplines finally helped me work through that impulsive behavior. I struggled with bulimia for years even after treatment; it was an on-and-off struggle; I guess I'm saying it was kind of like a coping mechanism I used for an emotional release. I would eat a bunch of unhealthy food on a road trip by myself and then stop to get rid of it. It was a very hard time in my life and in my recovery because I was using a non-drug substitute that was still very unhealthy.

I am healing well now, but that was what getting off drugs looked like for me. This journey will always be something that I will need to pray about and stay on top of with therapeutic language I speak to myself. I had to deal with a lot of core issues, and depending on drugs was just a symptom—something I used to maintain other emotional disordered things in my life. I am very thankful that I did find the importance of fitness early on in my recovery. That was kind of my go-to thing in treatment. I finally discovered my body type and how to train and fuel it properly. My plan of action includes exercise and movement every day to release endorphins (feel-good hormones) and to maintain my strength and physique. This keeps my mindset on the right track.

For me, treatment was an uncertain time and a freeing time. There were so many things going on with pretrial issues and going back and forth for court-related responsibilities. Plus, I was rebuilding relationships with family members and friends. I had to sign a paper in treatment saying I could have only supervised visits with my son, and this tore me apart. I was broken to the fullest and learned so much about myself in a three-month period.

The crazy thing about this was that I was just abruptly released back into the world after treatment and expected to maintain forward progress on my own. I'm so thankful that I had a wonderful support system straight out of the gate.

I was able to move in with my mom, and l got a wonderful job right away working in a treatment facility. It was the perfect fit because I was dealing with my own recovery and my own consequences for my actions. I was still involved in pretrial legal issues. I felt privileged to have a job in which I could mentor other young women in their recovery. It was such a blessing, and my employers were so accommodating for all the pretrial work I had to do.

I was able to see my son all the time, and he was able to stay with me on weekends at my mom's house. I would even sleep on my ex's couch to spend holidays with my son. It was so nice to start really growing a relationship with him. I got out of treatment when he was four.

There were many conditions of my pretrial during this time; for insistence, I did have to testify in federal court. One of my codefendants did not plead guilty to these crimes. We all had accepted the checks and cashed them and split the money, but one codefendant tried to convince the court that he had been owed the money through family inheritance. I was subpoenaed to testify, and I was questioned in front of a court of law. It was so scary, but also an experience I will never forget. I testified against a close friend of mine, which made it all even more difficult. I was the leading witness, and still in pretrial, so it was pretty much a requirement.

A little nerve-racking to say the least. I had not been clean for very long, so I was still having difficulty dealing with my emotions. I sure did learn a lot during that time about my capabilities, and I learned what not to be afraid of in life.

After I completed all my pretrial requirements, my mom and others spoke in front of the judge on my behalf and told him how much my life had changed. My mom spoke about how I had stayed on track and got a great job. I was sentenced to only two months in a women's camp and then three years of federal supervised release. At any point, I could be put back in prison to serve my probation time if I broke the conditions of my release. This kept me in check, and I had lots of people holding me accountable, including agents of the federal government.

I experienced a lot of growth during the first three years of my recovery because it all happened under federal supervision. I needed that accountability. After I was released, I had to check in every single week, and I had to call in every day on a color code. I had to check every day to see if I had to drive to Austin for a urine drug test. This kept me accountable and was helpful in keeping me off narcotics. I was also assigned nine months of outpatient group therapy and assigned to a one-on-one counselor whom I met with every week.

There were also many other factors that were keeping me clean. I had done the work while I was in treatment, so I had no desire to use meth anymore. My number-one reason for staying clean was my son and getting back my rights to see him. I was doing so much driving back and forth to Austin where he lived that I felt as if I could do it in my sleep. At first, I didn't have a car because I was broke and had the worst credit. So, I would catch the bus to downtown Austin anytime I wanted to see my son or had to see my probation officer. Then I would take a taxi back to the Greyhound station so I could get back on the bus to Brenham. Eventually, my mom trusted me enough to help me buy a car by cosigning a loan with me and helping me get insurance.

CHAPTER 7

The Steps with Jesus

When I got out of prison, I had every desire to start my life fresh. I did whatever hard thing I had to do to make up for all the wrongs I had done and to rebuild my life. Building something on top of an open hole isn't an easy task; a lot of foundation work must be done before anything can stand firm. As I said, I had rededicated my life to Jesus, so I decided I needed to do that fully. I now stand on that steady rock foundation.

Here I'd like to share with you the gospel passages that saved my life:

> Because, if you confess with your mouth that Jesus is Lord and believe in your heart that God raised him from the dead, you will be saved. For with the heart, one believes and is justified, and with the mouth one confesses and is saved. For the Scripture says, "Everyone who believes in him will not be put to shame." For there is no distinction between Jew and Greek; for the same Lord is Lord of all, bestowing his riches on all who call on him. For "everyone who calls on the name of the Lord will be saved.
> (Romans 10:9–13 ESV)

For God so loved the world, that he gave his only
Son, that whoever believes in him should not perish
but have eternal life.
(John 3:16 ESV)

And he said to them, "Go into all the world and
proclaim the gospel to the whole creation."
(Mark 16:15 ESV)

Now I would remind you, brothers, of the gospel
I preached to you, which you received, in which
you stand, and by which you are being saved, if you
hold fast to the word I preached to you—unless you
believed in vain. For I delivered to you as of first
importance what I also received: that Christ died
for our sins in accordance with the Scriptures, that
he was buried, that he was raised on the third day in
accordance with the Scriptures, and that he appeared
to Cephas, then to the twelve.
(1 Corinthians 15:1–28 ESV)

My life changed for good when I took the time to believe these
scriptures and admit that I needed help. Only then could I walk on
the path that led to a stable recovery. I decided to dedicate my life to
working to please God and following His law to love Him with all
my heart, soul, and mind, and to love my neighbors as I love myself.

I believe that Jesus Christ came to the world as fully God and
fully man to die on the cross to pay my penalty for not following
God's law and living a life of selfish drive. I believe that Jesus was
God in human form, and He lived a blameless life and resisted all
the temptations of this world. I believe He was killed for what He
was preaching about Himself, the Son of God. I believe that death
could not and will not hold Jesus Christ and that on the third day
after his death, He rose to live forever! The most wonderful thing I
believe and have hope in is that I am forgiven, and I will get to live

with Jesus forever in heaven. I know that, when I spread this message of hope to people, whoever believes in it will be saved from death just as I have been saved. Believe in this act that He did out of love for us humans, and you will get the most wonderful gift ever given. You will meet Jesus in the clouds one day. Having a little faith goes a long way, and it gives you a big amount of hope to go on each day.

> Be still and know that I am God. I will be exalted
> among the nations; I will be exalted in the earth!
> (Psalm 46:10 ESV)

I surrendered my life to Jesus and to obeying God's law. I walk with Him in my daily actions and pretty much talk to Him as though He is right here beside me. Because I believe that He is. I did this not because I felt I had to; I did it out of love and reverence for the Lord Almighty. I love Him because He helped me with my recovery and answered my desperate prayer. He helped get me into a treatment center because I asked. He provided a home for me when I got out, just as I had prayed for. I had prayed for transportation. I had prayed for a job and after care. I had prayed for my sentencing to be reduced. All these things were supplied for me. I was given a fantastic lawyer, and I was even able to get a job working for a treatment center to help young women who were recovering themselves. I was also given accountability with that program as well. I asked for the opportunity to go back to school and be able to have my own business. Done and done. I was given a Federal Pell Grants for college. I was able to own a coffee shop with my mom for years before I started my own health and fitness business.

I do remember having a conversation with God about not ever wanting to be in a relationship again. I told Him that my "picker" was broken. So, of course, God interpreted that as "Please send the perfect person for me so I can start my family." He took control of the picking. God had my future husband walk right into the gym where I worked as a side job in college. God is good and always supplies! He is there and listening. When I quit trying to rule my love life by going after lust, I was able to see what kind of relationship God had planned for me.

If you seek Him with your whole heart and pray without ceasing, He is there to handle all your needs. He even throws in many blessings along the way. I was blessed with a family-in-law who are godly and real Christians. They model Christ and have taught me so much. My husband loves and fears the Lord, and his dad was a strong father figure to him. He models this every day with the beautiful son we were blessed with. My mother-in-law and sister-in-law are two of the strongest women I know, and they always work hard to serve our family and the community. They are fantastic mentors to me and show me what God wants from us as women. As He says in Proverbs 31, this is the kind of woman I want to be to my family. This is a fantastic model that we can strive for. My husband's grandmother taught so many women to strive for this type of servitude. Grannie will always be that special someone who gave me that special attention and saw something in me. She welcomed me into her family when I married her grandson as if I had no past problems at all. She showed me the love of Christ from the first second she met me. It was as if I had no troubles on that day and, indeed, had never had troubles in the past. She was the most nonjudgmental but straightforward woman I have ever met. She was such a wise woman, and she helped so many young women who were on their journeys into motherhood and life and business. She owned multiple successful businesses and employed hard-working people who wanted to learn. She was a major donor in the community and gave up her time and energy until the day she died. She truly did model what it was to be a Proverbs 31 woman. I will always be very grateful for the role models I was given when I rededicated my life to the Lord.

I have been able to rebuild a good relationship with my adult son, and we get closer every year. God is moving in his life and growing him into a strong young man of God! I have also been able to reconnect to lost family members who were pushed away because of my addictions.

I have been shown so much mercy and grace by so many people.

But most importantly, I was given forgiveness and mercy by the Lord God through the blood of Jesus Christ, His Son! God has handled and made a way for me to handle all my debt here on earth and in heaven.

When I was pregnant with my second son, I said a prayer about getting out of debt. I prayed that I wouldn't have to deal with the penalties anymore from my past life. I prayed this debt would be taken care of and I could be done with it. I wanted it to go away! This debt that I owed was for court costs and restitution to the federal government. I was paying $100 a month and was set to do that for years and years until it was paid off. I would still be paying it today. But after I said that prayer, I got my last check back and a letter saying that my debt was at zero. This gives me chills just saying it, but I know that God took away that debt. It was over $32,000 one day, and the next day it was zero! When I called everyone in the legal departments, they all said it had been paid in full by others involved. All my codefendants were responsible for the court cost part of that, and that cost had been paid in full. I know it was a God thing because the legal department workers didn't have any other information to give me regarding the subject.

God just handles things when I least expect it. He works in ways I can't even imagine or explain. I must pray, and I must believe with my whole heart. The Bible says, if I have faith even as small as a mustard seed, I can move mountains. I know this to be true because He has moved huge mountains in my life. God has blessed me with a wonderful life on earth as it is in heaven!

I was blessed with a family that has taught me so much. They taught me what a beautiful loving family who loves God looks like. My father God has made a way for me to serve and help others who are lost and need help. He has made a way for those who need to hear the good news of Jesus and His death to be able to hear it.

We all have made our own life mistakes; we all need a chance to hear this message of hope and to heal. In God, we are given a hope in Christ for eternal life. With that hope comes no fear of the future or of death. Death can no longer hold me, just as it could not hold

Christ. I have eternal life in heaven. The good news is that we are loved. We were loved even while we were breaking all the laws! We are not following God to the fullest of obedience! Nobody is perfect like God! I will die in that if it continues. God is a merciful God and full of patience. He wants us all to live with Him as He intended in the Garden of Eden.

God loved us so much that He sent His only Son to be born of a virgin and to live a perfect life. Jesus showed us how to do it, only to be killed for preaching about this news. Jesus knew He was dying, and He gave His life out of love for *all* of us! Without the belief in Jesus, I was dying! Jesus loved me enough to make sure that I knew of His love and really felt Him with me. He saved me from that death. He did it on the cross that day! He has forgiven me and conquered death for me! Three days later, He rose again. I prayed for help, and He showed up for me three days later! I believe that God works in cool ways to show me that I am not alone.

I must seek Him daily in the Word of God. Open your Bible and read the books of John, Luke, Proverbs, and Psalms for the praises. God speaks to me through His Word. Jesus is a gift. Each person must receive Him for herself or himself. Jesus died, and all we must do is accept it and follow Him. Jesus came for the sick. If you come as you are, He will do the rest!

When we ask Jesus to forgive us for the decisions we've made that do not follow along with what God says He wants for us, we are forgiven and those sins are forgotten. Have faith in Jesus's live, His death, and His resurrection and return. With this faith, you are given eternal life with the Lord! With this faith comes growth, and we become a new creature in Christ! If I seek His face in all I do, He will show Himself in everything I do.

> Blessed are those who wash their robes, so that they
> may have the right to the tree of life and that they
> may enter the city by the gates.
> (Revelation 22:14 ESV)

CHAPTER 8

Jesus is the Game Changer—This is the Way I See Him Now

Jesus promised to pay the cost; He came down and walked in the flesh—God in flesh through His Son. God needs us to be right with no sin. We can't do that because we are human. So, Jesus was sent to pay the cost. Jesus will meet you where you are in your sickness and in your hurt. He is here to heal you and to love you through it. Jesus was hated, and the sins of the earth killed Him. But death could not hold Jesus. He was alive in three days, and I have learned that, when I receive this story and believe it to be true, I am saved forever and get to spend eternal life with our Lord and Savior, the Almighty.

I walk daily to grow and maintain my gifts

My heart, soul, and mind have been surrounding these teachings, and I strive and pray to be more pleasing to God every day. My mission is to share how my pain and sickness were turned into the glory of God. My mission is to help others believe that God has an awesome plan for them through His Son, Jesus Christ. I have been blessed with a job in health and fitness. I am able to help others correct some of the stinking thinking about food and exercise. I get to help with empowering and guiding others with Christ by working with the youth in our community. I get to spread the love and the good news of the message of hope to help them feel the healthiest and strongest while they are still on the earth doing the work they need to do. I hope to help other lives get easier and prosper through the gifts that God has given me. I hope to help others find their gifts.

But then we are not to be anxious about it either, as stated in Luke.

> And he said to his disciples, Therefore I tell you, do not anxious about your life, what you will eat, nor about your body, what you will put on. For life is more than food, and the body more than clothing. Consider the ravens: they neither sow nor reap, they have neither storehouse nor barn, and yet God feeds them. Of how more value you than the birds!
>
> (Luke 12:22-24 ESV)

When we ask God for balance and the freedom to rest in Him, we can do all things through Him. Know that our strength comes from Christ. Your self-control comes from God. All your spiritual gifts and fruit were given to you by the One Who created you, and He intended for you to use them. Teach others that, if they pray to the One Who Is and created you to be, you will be strong and healthy and live in His will. Know that no weapon formed against you can stand and that you are undefeated in Christ. Serve God with your body; make it the best it can be for Him who made you.

> Therefore, I urge you, brothers, by the mercies of God, to present your bodies a living sacrifice, holy, acceptable to God, which is your spiritual service.
>
> (Romans 12:1 WEB)

God wants you to put away the nasty, unhealthy dark stuff and fill your mind and heart with what is good and what serves God. We are challenged in God's Word to glorify Him with our bodies. Read 1 Corinthians 6:19–20. It feels good to be free from the conforming world! Free to give your Heavenly Father all your pain, hurt, struggle, weight, stress, and all that is negative in life. When you do this, God can turn it around for good. Your turnaround is God's glory. He takes care of your needs and makes all things possible for you who have belief in Him. All it takes is faith as small as a mustard seed to make all things possible through prayer to God (Matthew 17:20).

Whatever happens in your life, you can trust and believe in these promises given to you by God. If you stick to your part of believing that God is in control over your life, He will stick to His promise of holding you tight forever. Promises given by God are what you hold fast, knowing that death can't hold those who follow Christ.

I repeat this to myself when I need to be reminded: "I am alive in Christ, and that eternity started when I accepted that gift. Yes, a gift of eternal salvation in heaven. I am confident in that, and I will share your experiences with someone else." This is The good news that needs to be shared.

Let God's will be done. Spread His message to the nations. Live life in the Light always!

Thank you for listening to how Jesus saved my life by answering a simple prayer. He answered my prayer of repentance and acceptance when I was a young child, and He never left my side. He protected me from myself when I was weak. He cleaned me up when I asked for help. He set my feet on solid ground and gave me ways to serve Him. He loves me, and I feel that through His many blessings and through the love He has shown through others in my life. I believe that my struggle and victories in Christ are what built my spiritual muscle for what God still has planned for my life. My hope is that you trust in Him. Do this, and He will show you His plans for you.

Here is a poem I wrote. I like to think about this when times are difficult:

On solid ground I grow.
My branches become so strong as they bear the storm.
I even bear more fruit.
I will produce a strong seed.

The storm will scatter them.
The storm will water them.
Growth occurs and multiplies life.

May God bless your life as well!
With so much love,
Sarah Bevers

> Heal me, O Lord, and I shall be healed; save me, and I shall be saved, for You are my praise.
> (Jeremiah 17:14 ESV)

> So, flee youthful passions and pursue righteousness, faith, love, and peace, along with those who call on the Lord from a pure heart.
> (2 Timothy 2:22 ESV)

> He who testifies to these things says, "Surely I am coming quickly." Amen. Even so, come, Lord Jesus! The grace of our Lord Jesus Christ be with you all. Amen.
> (Revelation 22:20-21 NKJV)

BOOKS THAT CAN HELP YOU THROUGH YOUR WALK

- NKJV, *Study Bible*
- *Created to Be His Help Meet: Discover how God can make your marriage glorious* by Debi Pearl
- *Narcotics Anonymous* by World Services Organization (WSO)
- *Jesus Calling: Enjoying Peace in His Presence* (with Scripture References) by Sarah Young
- *My Utmost for His Highest: Classic Language* (Gift Edition) by Oswald Chambers
- *Create a Better Brain through Neuroplasticity: A Manual for Mamas* by Debi Pearl
- *PUSH: 30 Days to Turbocharged Habits, a Bangin' Body, and the Life You Deserve!* by Chalene Johnson
- *Smartlife Push Journal* by Chalene Johnson
- *131 Method: Your Personalized Nutrition Solution to Boost Metabolism, Restore Gut Health, and Lose Weight* by Chalene Johnson
- *High Performance Habits: How Extraordinary People Become That Way* by Brendon Burchard
- Atomic Habits: An Easy & Proven Way to Build Good Habits & Break Bad Ones by James Clear
- *How to Win Friends & Influence People* by Dale Carnegie

Printed in the United States
by Baker & Taylor Publisher Services